Scary Russian History Facts

CRAFTED BY SKRIUWER

Copyright © 2025 by Skriuwer.

All rights reserved. No part of this book may be used or reproduced in any form whatsoever without written permission except in the case of brief quotations in critical articles or reviews.

At **Skriuwer**, we're more than just a team—we're a global community of people who love books. In Frisian, "Skriuwer" means "writer," and that's at the heart of what we do: creating and sharing books with readers worldwide. Wherever you are in the world, **Skriuwer** is here to inspire learning.

Frisian is one of the oldest languages in Europe, closely related to English and Dutch, and is spoken by about **500,000 people** in the province of **Friesland** (Fryslân), located in the northern Netherlands. It's the second official language of the Netherlands, but like many minority languages, Frisian faces the challenge of survival in a modern, globalized world.

We're using the money we earn to promote the Frisian language.

For more information, contact : **kontakt@skriuwer.com** (www.skriuwer.com)

Disclaimer:
The images in this book are creative reinterpretations of historical scenes. While every effort was made to accurately capture the essence of the periods depicted, some illustrations may include artistic embellishments or approximations. They are intended to evoke the atmosphere and spirit of the times rather than serve as precise historical records.

TABLE OF CONTENTS

CHAPTER 1: EARLY SLAVIC ORIGINS AND THE RISE OF KIEVAN RUS

- *Foundations of early Slavic tribes*
- *Influence of Norse (Varangians) on local communities*
- *Formation of a united Rus under strong leaders*

CHAPTER 2: THE MONGOL INVASION AND ITS HORRORS

- *Destruction of major Rus cities and mass violence*
- *Heavy tributes and the long-lasting "Mongol Yoke"*
- *Emergence of Moscow as a focal point for recovery*

CHAPTER 3: THE RISE OF MUSCOVY AND THE EMERGENCE OF IVAN THE TERRIBLE

- *End of the Mongol rule and Moscow's growing power*
- *Ivan's early reforms and territorial expansion*
- *Introduction of the Oprichnina and fear-based governance*

CHAPTER 4: THE TIME OF TROUBLES AND FALSE TSARS

- *Succession crises after Ivan the Terrible's death*
- *Rise of pretenders to the throne (False Dmitrys)*
- *Widespread famine and social breakdown*

CHAPTER 5: THE EARLY ROMANOVS AND THE HARSH LIFE OF SERFS

- *Restoration of order under the Romanov family*
- *Tightening of serfdom and peasant struggles*
- *Efforts to stabilize a war-ravaged land*

CHAPTER 6: PETER THE GREAT'S REFORMS AND METHODS OF CONTROL

- *Forced westernization and modernization*
- *Building of St. Petersburg through brutal labor*
- *Centralizing power and subduing noble opposition*

CHAPTER 7: EMPRESS ELIZABETH, CATHERINE THE GREAT, AND COURT INTRIGUE

- *Intricate palace plots and power shifts*
- *Catherine's expansionist policies and Enlightenment ideas*
- *Continuing the harsh treatment of serfs and rebels*

CHAPTER 8: PUGACHEV'S REBELLION AND THE WIDENING GULF BETWEEN CLASSES

- *Largest peasant uprising of its time*
- *Rebel violence and government crackdowns*
- *Stricter control over serfs after the revolt*

CHAPTER 9: PAUL I'S TURBULENT REIGN AND RUTHLESS POLICIES

- *Unpredictable leadership and strict military regulations*
- *Alienation of nobility and common people*
- *Paul's assassination and its immediate aftermath*

CHAPTER 10: THE WAR OF 1812 AND THE MISERY IT LEFT BEHIND

- *Napoleon's invasion and the burning of Moscow*
- *Widespread hunger and devastation in rural areas*
- *Emergence of Russian nationalism amid suffering*

CHAPTER 11: NICHOLAS I AND THE ERA OF STRICT SURVEILLANCE

- *Expansion of secret police and censorship*
- *Enforcement of the "Official Nationality" doctrine*
- *Growing restlessness among intellectuals and peasants*

CHAPTER 12: THE CRIMEAN WAR AND ITS LASTING DAMAGE

- *Military defeats and shortages on the front lines*
- *Economic strain and loss of international prestige*
- *Calls for reform in the wake of failures*

CHAPTER 13: ALEXANDER II'S REFORMS AND VIOLENT RESPONSES

- *Emancipation of the serfs and its limitations*
- *Rise of radical groups and assassinations*
- *Balancing modernization with internal resistance*

CHAPTER 14: THE RISE OF REVOLUTIONARY IDEAS UNDER ALEXANDER III

- *Crackdowns on dissent and increased police powers*
- *Suppression of national minorities and liberal movements*
- *Formation of underground revolutionary cells*

CHAPTER 15: HARDSHIPS IN FACTORIES AND FIELDS, AND THE DARK SIDE OF INDUSTRIAL GROWTH

- *Exploitative working conditions and child labor*
- *Peasant poverty and frequent crop failures*
- *Early worker strikes and their brutal suppression*

CHAPTER 16: THE RUSSO-JAPANESE WAR AND THE BLOODY SUNDAY TRAGEDY

- *Military defeat and national humiliation*
- *Unrest fueled by economic misery and ethnic tensions*
- *Peaceful protest turned massacre outside the Winter Palace*

CHAPTER 17: THE ROLE OF SECRET POLICE AND THE SHADOW OF EXILE

- *Expansion of the Okhrana's surveillance and infiltration*
- *Exile of political opponents to remote Siberian camps*
- *Fear and paranoia shaping daily life*

CHAPTER 18: THE SPREAD OF REVOLUTIONARY TERROR AND GOVERNMENT RETALIATION

- *Bombings and assassinations by radical factions*
- *Harsh crackdown on suspected revolutionaries*
- *Cycle of violence between activists and authorities*

CHAPTER 19: THE FINAL DAYS OF THE ROMANOV DYNASTY

- *Mounting economic crisis and social unrest*
- *Rasputin's influence and court scandals*
- *Increasingly desperate attempts to maintain control*

CHAPTER 20: A LEGACY OF FEAR AND OPPRESSION

- *Reflection on centuries of violence and strict rule*
- *How historical terror shaped political power structures*
- *Enduring lessons from Russia's unsettling past*

CHAPTER 1

EARLY SLAVIC ORIGINS AND THE RISE OF KIEVAN RUS

Introduction

Russia's roots go back to the early Slavic tribes who lived in the vast forests and plains of Eastern Europe. Over time, these tribes formed various groups, each with its own customs and ways of survival. Life in these regions could be harsh. Winters were cold, and communities often faced threats from raiders or rival tribes. In such a setting, survival meant strong leadership and unity. The story of how these scattered groups began to unite under a more centralized rule is key to understanding the early roots of Russia.

The Slavic world included tribes that stretched from the Baltic region in the north to the Black Sea in the south. As these groups grew in size, they started building fortified settlements and trading with neighbors. Some of the tribes formed alliances, which helped them defend their lands against invaders. One crucial development was the involvement of Norse traders and warriors, often called Varangians or Vikings. These foreign figures arrived in the region, bringing new military tactics and systems of governance. Over time, the blend of Slavic and Norse traditions created the powerful state we know as Kievan Rus.

This chapter explores the everyday realities of these early times and the foundations of Kievan Rus. We will look at how trade routes shaped the region, what kind of rulers rose to power, and how ordinary people lived. We will also see the darker side of this era—constant warfare, kidnappings, and the harsh punishments used to maintain order. It was a world of shifting alliances and fear, a world where entire villages could be wiped out in a single raid. Through this lens, we can see how fragile life was for the ancestors of today's Russians.

The Slavic Tribes and Their World

The Slavs who lived in the forests and steppes had to cope with a variety of challenges. Dense woodlands offered some shelter from enemies, but they also limited farming. Steppes in the south provided more open space but left communities vulnerable to raids from nomadic groups. Because of these geographical difficulties, the Slavs developed strong communal bonds. Clans shared resources and built wooden forts. Within these forts, members could find protection, but they also had to follow strict rules to survive.

Most Slavic people lived off agriculture, growing crops like wheat, barley, and rye. They also kept livestock, hunted for game, and fished in nearby rivers. Life was not easy; failing crops or harsh winters could bring famine. Disease often spread quickly through close-knit settlements. Knowledge of medicine was limited, so even small injuries could become life-threatening. In some communities, punishments for disobeying local customs were severe, including banishment or worse. Fear of the unknown shaped a world where many worshiped a mix of gods tied to nature.

Early Conflicts and Tribal Warfare

Tribal warfare was common. Disputes arose over grazing land, trading routes, and resources like furs or salt. Losing a battle could mean the destruction of entire villages. Warriors would sometimes take captives to sell as slaves, or they might perform raids just to scare rivals. During these times, horror stories spread. It was not unusual to hear tales of violence and cruelty. Some tribes displayed the heads of enemies on stakes to warn others. These acts were meant to instill fear and prevent future attacks. Such methods left a mark on collective memory, passing down a sense that life was fragile and dangerous.

The Norse Influence and the Varangians

Around the 9th century, Norse explorers and traders, often referred to as Varangians, traveled along the rivers that linked the Baltic Sea and the Black Sea. They used these rivers for trade, exchanging goods like furs, wax, and honey from the north for silk, spices, and other products from the Byzantine Empire and beyond. Over time, some of these Norse leaders became rulers over the local Slavic populations.

One of the most famous figures is Rurik, a Varangian chieftain who is said to have taken control of Novgorod in the mid-9th century. Under Rurik and his successors, a form of centralized power began to emerge. Tribes that once fought each other found themselves under the authority of these Norse rulers. Though these leaders brought a sense of order, they also demanded tributes and labor. Their rule was not always gentle. Local populations that resisted might face brutal crackdowns.

Formation of Kievan Rus

By the late 9th century, Rurik's relative, Oleg, moved south to the city of Kiev. He seized control of Kiev from local rulers, creating a new center of power. This entity, known as Kievan Rus, would go on to dominate the region for centuries. Kiev's location along major trade routes turned it into a wealthy city. Tribes were expected to pay tribute to Kiev, which financed armies and monumental building projects, such as wooden palaces and early churches.

However, with wealth also came conflict. Local chieftains wanted autonomy, and some refused to submit to the grand prince in Kiev. Tax collectors were sometimes attacked or murdered. Armies had to be sent to keep regions in line. In these campaigns, villages that resisted were often burned, and survivors were made an example of. Tales of these destructive attacks spread, and people learned that opposing Kiev's rule could bring disastrous consequences.

Everyday Life in Kievan Rus

Despite these risks, Kievan Rus grew in influence. Trade brought new goods, religions, and ideas. Many rulers found it useful to align themselves with powerful states, such as the Byzantine Empire. But for the ordinary person, life was still tough. Most people worked on farms or engaged in small trade. In times of famine, they relied on stored grain if they were lucky enough to have it. A bad harvest often led to hunger, disease, and a rise in crime. Thieves might steal food or livestock, and desperate people sometimes turned to banditry.

Justice could be swift and harsh. A local lord or prince might order punishments that included mutilation, whipping, or execution. There was no formal prison system as we know it today, so public punishments served as a method of control. Fear kept many in line. Yet, religion also started to play a more significant role in daily life. Pagan beliefs were widespread, but contact with the Byzantines introduced Christianity. Some early Christian missionaries preached love and forgiveness, but acceptance of their message took time.

The Influence of Religion

Once Christianity took hold in Kievan Rus, especially after the conversion of Prince Vladimir the Great in the late 10th century, it brought both spiritual comfort and social control. Churches were built, and the clergy gained influence. Religious texts taught obedience to rulers. The church also promoted moral codes, but these codes could be used to justify punishing anyone seen as a threat to social order. The peasants often welcomed church holidays because they provided breaks from farm work, but they also had to support the church through various forms of tribute. For many, religion was a double-edged sword—a source of hope and fear.

Political Struggles and Succession Wars

After the Christianization, Kievan Rus continued to grow, but it was never fully united under one strong ruler for very long. Princes fought each other for the grand throne in Kiev. They also competed for control over other prosperous cities like Novgorod, Polotsk, and Vladimir. These battles led to shifting alliances, betrayals, and assassinations. If a prince suspected he might lose power, he would imprison, blind, or kill rivals, including relatives.

Ordinary people suffered in these power struggles. Armies marched across farmlands, seizing crops and livestock. Taxes increased to fund wars. When princes fell, entire families could be exiled or massacred. Chronicles from this period mention the terror that local populations felt, never knowing when a new conflict might flare up. Some towns tried to remain neutral, but that was difficult when princes and their rivals demanded loyalty.

Conclusion

The rise of Kievan Rus was not a gentle process. It involved military conquest, harsh reprisals, and heavy taxation. For every new church or market that opened in Kiev or Novgorod, many villages felt the weight of tribute and fear. The legacy of the early Slavs and the influence of the Norse set the stage for a society that would continue to struggle with central authority. This blend of violence, religion, and the quest for power would shape Russia for generations to come.

Kievan Rus would achieve a golden age under certain rulers, leading to growth in art, culture, and trade. Yet, behind the scenes, the threat of raids, family feuds, and external wars loomed large. This era laid the groundwork for the future. As we move forward to the Mongol invasion and beyond, we will see how the seeds planted during this early period grew into a complex and often frightening story. The cautionary tales from these early days remind us of how fragile life and power can be, and how fear was used as a tool of control from the very beginning of Russian history.

CHAPTER 2

THE MONGOL INVASION AND ITS HORRORS

Introduction

In the first chapter, we explored how Kievan Rus formed and saw how violence and power struggles shaped its early years. But no event would test the strength of Kievan Rus more severely than the Mongol invasion. In the mid-13th century, the Mongols swept across the steppes, targeting major cities. Their impact was devastating. Towns were burned to the ground, populations were slaughtered or enslaved, and surviving princes were forced to pay heavy tribute to the Mongol khans. This period, often called the "Mongol Yoke," changed the fate of the region forever.

The Mongol Empire, created by Genghis Khan and expanded by his descendants, was highly organized. Mongol armies were known for their exceptional horsemanship and military tactics. They utilized siege engines and psychological warfare. They were also known for their brutality against those who resisted. Stories of entire cities wiped from the map spread far and wide, instilling fear in many populations even before the Mongols arrived. Kievan Rus was not prepared for such a powerful foe. Divisions among the Rus princes made it even easier for the invaders to conquer large portions of the land.

This chapter takes a closer look at the Mongol invasion, the resulting terror, and how it forever changed the political, social, and cultural landscape of Rus. We will discuss the fall of key cities, the mass devastation, the tribute system, and the lasting grip the Mongols had on local rulers. We will also explore how local populations tried to survive under such harsh conditions. This era cast a long shadow, shaping Russian history in grim ways.

The Mongol War Machine

Under the leadership of Genghis Khan, the Mongols conquered a vast empire stretching from China to Eastern Europe. After Genghis Khan's death, his descendants continued to push westward. The Mongol war machine was efficient and terrifying. Skilled archers on horseback could maneuver quickly, encircle enemy troops, and launch volleys of arrows. If a city or settlement resisted, the Mongols often responded with merciless violence.

When the Mongols reached the principalities of Rus, they encountered a region that was politically fragmented. While some princes tried to unite, deep rivalries and previous wars had weakened their forces. The Mongols, led by Batu Khan (a grandson of Genghis Khan), launched a campaign in 1237 that would bring much of the area under Mongol control.

The Siege of Ryazan

One of the first major cities to face the Mongols was Ryazan. The siege began in December 1237. According to chronicles, the city's leaders begged for help from nearby principalities, but none came in time. The Mongols surrounded Ryazan and attacked relentlessly. They used catapults and battering rams to breach the city's walls. Once inside, they set fires and slaughtered anyone who resisted. Women and children were taken captive. The entire city was left in ruins.

Ryazan's fall sent shockwaves throughout Kievan Rus. Other cities realized they might be next. Some tried to fortify their defenses, while others fled. Refugees with horrible stories of the Mongol attacks poured into neighboring regions. Their tales included children being torn from their parents, entire families burned alive in churches, and massive fields of the dead. Fear was the Mongols' most effective weapon, and it worked.

Attempted Resistance and More Defeats

After Ryazan fell, the Mongols continued, taking Kolomna and then moving towards Moscow. Moscow was a smaller town at the time, but it, too, fell quickly to the invaders. The Mongols then set their sights on Vladimir, a key city. Vladimir's prince, Yuri II, tried to gather an army but did not arrive in time to save the city. The Mongols used the same tactics—siege, bombardment, entry, and destruction.

Despite these devastating defeats, some pockets of resistance formed. Princes from the north attempted to join forces, and local militias were created. But none of these efforts matched the organization and sheer force of the Mongol horde. One by one, major cities like Suzdal and Rostov fell or submitted. The

Mongols' practice of sparing those who quickly surrendered (in exchange for high tribute) also encouraged many leaders to submit without a fight, hoping to save their lands from destruction.

The Fall of Kiev

By 1240, the Mongols reached Kiev, the jewel of Rus and a major religious center. Kiev had already been weakened by internal strife and previous attacks. Still, its defenders tried to fight off the Mongols. But Batu Khan's forces were simply too strong. After a brutal siege, Kiev fell. Most of its buildings were destroyed, including churches. Many people were killed or taken as slaves. The once-grand city lay in ruins, and its downfall symbolized the end of Kievan Rus as a major power.

This event is often seen as one of the darkest moments in Russian history. Chronicles describe streets filled with corpses and the Dnieper River red with blood. Churches that once stood as symbols of faith and learning were burned to the ground, their icons and sacred items looted. Surviving monks wrote about the invasion in desperate language, describing it as a punishment from God or an act of divine wrath. Fear, despair, and hopelessness were widespread.

Life Under the Mongols

With the fall of Kiev and other key cities, the Mongols established their rule over the Rus territories. They set up a system of tribute collection, forcing princes to travel to the Mongol capital (known as the Golden Horde) to receive their titles from the khan. This gave the khan the power to approve or reject any prince. Princes who displeased the Mongols risked losing their positions—or their heads.

The people under Mongol rule faced heavy taxes. Collectors, sometimes accompanied by Mongol soldiers, would arrive in villages and demand payment in silver, grain, livestock, or slaves. If payments were not made on time, the collectors might burn the village or enslave its inhabitants. This cycle created a climate of constant fear. Additionally, the Mongols demanded soldiers from the local population for their armies, leading many families to see their sons taken away, often never to return.

Economic Burden and Social Changes

The tribute system drained resources, preventing economic recovery for many regions. Craftsmen who might have helped rebuild cities were forced to work for the Mongols or fled to safer areas. Trade routes were disrupted by war, although some Mongol policies did encourage long-distance commerce later on. But for the average peasant, life was bleak. Houses destroyed in invasions took years to rebuild, if they were rebuilt at all. Famine sometimes followed because farmland was ruined or because Mongol demands left little for local consumption.

Socially, the Mongol Yoke also shifted power balances among local princes. Those who cooperated with the Mongols could grow stronger, as they received the khan's support in rivalries with other princes. Over time, the princes of Moscow learned to use this cooperation to gain favor. They became key collectors of Mongol tribute, which increased their influence. This laid the foundation for Moscow's eventual rise, but that process came at the expense of many others who suffered under the Mongol system.

Religious Tolerance and Control

Interestingly, the Mongols were relatively tolerant of different religions. They allowed the Orthodox Church to function, seeing it as a way to keep the population calm. In return, church leaders prayed for the khan's health and cooperated with the Mongol authorities. The church's status was often respected, so church lands and property were sometimes spared from destruction. This tolerance helped the church survive and even become more influential. People turned to religious leaders for hope during these terrible times.

However, this tolerance did not lessen the constant threat of violence. The Mongols remained focused on maintaining order and collecting tribute. If a region failed to pay, no amount of religious ties could save it. Church leaders sometimes tried to negotiate on behalf of their flock, but their success was limited. The Mongols cared more about loyalty and payment than faith.

Resistance Efforts and Brutal Reprisals

Over the decades, there were attempts to rebel against Mongol rule. Some princes allied with neighboring powers like Lithuania or Poland, hoping to push out the invaders. Occasionally, a local leader would refuse to collect tribute, or villagers would kill Mongol tax collectors. These acts led to severe punishment. The Mongols would send an army to lay waste to an entire region, killing or enslaving thousands as a warning to others.

Tales of such reprisals spread quickly. Stories of mass executions, forced marches of prisoners, and widespread looting discouraged many from resisting. Even in rare cases where rebels achieved a small victory, the Mongols almost always returned with a larger force. This pattern of rebellion followed by brutal crackdown became a tragic cycle. The people learned that open resistance usually led to greater suffering.

The Lasting Impact

The Mongol Yoke lasted for more than two centuries. It delayed many forms of cultural and economic development. While Western Europe was experiencing growth in trade and the early stirrings of the Renaissance, the Rus lands were under foreign domination. The constant burden of tribute and fear stifled innovation. Schools and libraries that might have flourished were instead neglected or destroyed. Many skilled workers and artisans either died or relocated.

But the Mongol influence was not purely destructive. Over time, the Rus adopted certain military techniques and administrative methods from the Mongols. For example, the practice of keeping detailed records of tribute collection influenced later Russian administrative systems. Some argue that the centralized power structure that developed in Russia was partly shaped by Mongol methods of control. Rulers like the princes of Moscow learned to be both diplomats and fearsome enforcers, qualities they used to consolidate power.

Emergence of Moscow

One of the surprising outcomes of the Mongol invasion was the rise of Moscow. Initially a minor town, Moscow grew in importance by cooperating with the Mongols. Its princes acted as reliable tax collectors. Over time, they gained

17

wealth and political clout. When the Mongols began to weaken due to internal strife and external pressures, the princes of Moscow saw an opportunity. By the late 14th century, rulers like Dmitry Donskoy began to challenge Mongol authority, winning symbolic victories such as the Battle of Kulikovo in 1380, though Mongol rule did not end immediately.

Eventually, under Grand Prince Ivan III, Moscow threw off Mongol control entirely in 1480 at the Ugra River standoff. This marked the start of a new era, with Moscow at the center of a unified Russian state. Yet, the scars of the Mongol Yoke remained. The memory of those dark days did not fade quickly. The harsh treatment, the tribute, and the fear had taught Russian rulers how to enforce authority. Many historians argue that Russia's later inclination toward autocratic rule can be partly traced back to the Mongol period, when centralized power and fear-based control became deeply ingrained in the political culture.

Conclusion

The Mongol invasion was one of the most terrifying chapters in Russian history. Cities like Ryazan, Vladimir, and Kiev were reduced to ash. Thousands were killed, enslaved, or forced to pay heavy tribute. The event reshaped the course of Rus, wiping out the dominance of Kiev and paving the way for Moscow's eventual rise. The Mongols were masters of psychological and physical warfare, using fear to maintain control. This fear and domination lasted for more than two hundred years, impacting daily life, politics, and culture.

Under the Mongols, the Rus principalities learned lessons about centralized power and ruthless efficiency. Though the Mongols eventually faded as a controlling force, their legacy remained. The devastation and trauma they inflicted lived on in folk tales and chronicles, serving as a warning of what could happen when a powerful, united enemy attacks a divided land.

As we move forward in this book, we will see how the consolidation of power in Moscow set the stage for future rulers, including Ivan the Terrible. The methods of control and intimidation developed during the Mongol era influenced later autocrats. Through these experiences, fear continued to play a major role in Russian governance and society, reinforcing the pattern of strict rule and limited freedoms for the common people. The lesson was clear: unity might bring strength, but division could lead to unimaginable horror—a lesson passed down through the generations of Russian history.

CHAPTER 3

THE RISE OF MUSCOVY AND THE EMERGENCE OF IVAN THE TERRIBLE

Introduction

The Mongol invasion had left most of the Rus principalities in ruins. Major cities like Kiev had been devastated, and local rulers were reduced to paying heavy tribute. However, amidst the ruins, one principality steadily rose to prominence: Muscovy (also known as the Grand Duchy of Moscow). Over the course of the 14th and 15th centuries, Muscovy's princes learned how to work with the Mongols while also plotting to regain full independence. This balancing act made them both wealthy and influential.

As time passed, Moscow's leaders grew bolder. They collected tribute on behalf of the Mongols but kept a share for themselves. They secured alliances, married into important families, and expanded their territories. By the reign of Ivan III, often called Ivan the Great, Moscow had largely thrown off Mongol control, setting the stage for a unified Russian state. After Ivan III, the line continued through Vasili III and eventually to Ivan IV—better known to history as Ivan the Terrible. Under Ivan IV, Muscovy evolved into the Tsardom of Russia, expanding its frontiers while also descending into internal terror.

In this chapter, we will explore how the princes of Moscow outmaneuvered rivals and overcame the Mongols. We will see how Ivan the Great laid the foundations of a centralized Russian state. Then, we will examine Ivan the Terrible's early reforms, his brutal campaign against the nobility (the boyars), and the formation of the Oprichnina. Behind the rise of a powerful Russia, there were dreadful realities—executions, torture, forced relocations, and widespread fear. Ivan the Terrible's methods would echo across Russian history, leaving a legacy of control by fear and violence.

Muscovy's Path to Power

After the Mongols took over much of the Rus lands in the 13th century, the region was divided into various principalities. Each local prince had limited autonomy, but all had to recognize the authority of the Mongol Khan and pay tribute. Moscow, at first, was not the biggest or the most powerful of these regions. Cities like Tver and Novgorod held more prestige. However, the princes of Moscow proved especially skillful in navigating Mongol politics.

Cooperation and Opportunism

Moscow's rulers would go to the Golden Horde's capital to receive official titles, showing loyalty to the Khan. At the same time, they worked to undermine rival cities. They collected tribute on behalf of the Mongols, winning the Khan's favor, yet they also kept part of the tribute, enriching themselves. When a rival prince fell out of favor with the Khan, Moscow's leaders swooped in to gain new territories or privileges. Little by little, their lands expanded.

One of the earliest figures to push Moscow forward was Prince Ivan I, often called Ivan Kalita ("Moneybags"). He used his position as a favored tax collector to amass great wealth. He also encouraged the Orthodox Church to move its headquarters to Moscow, boosting the city's status as a religious center. Where Kiev once held spiritual leadership, Moscow gradually took over. The city's population grew, and its fortifications improved. Ivan I's successors continued the policy of balancing loyalty to the Mongols with steady territorial growth.

Dmitry Donskoy and the Battle of Kulikovo

A key moment in Moscow's rise was the Battle of Kulikovo in 1380. Dmitry Ivanovich, known as Dmitry Donskoy, led a Russian force against a Mongol army on the Kulikovo Field. Although the Mongols were not entirely driven out after this battle, it was a symbolic victory. It showed that the Mongols could be defeated. Dmitry Donskoy's reputation soared, and many Rus principalities looked to Moscow for leadership.

However, this did not end Mongol rule overnight. The Mongols returned later, sacking Moscow in retaliation. Yet the idea of a united Russian force under Moscow's leadership had taken root. The seeds of a more powerful state were planted.

Ivan III (Ivan the Great) and Independence

By the time Ivan III took the throne in 1462, Moscow was well on its way to becoming the dominant power in the region. Ivan III pursued a policy of unifying the Rus lands under his control. He conquered or annexed neighboring principalities, sometimes by war, sometimes by marriage. As his territories expanded, so did his ambition.

In 1478, Ivan III took over the Republic of Novgorod, a wealthy city known for its strong trading ties. Novgorod had been a center of relative freedom and local governance, but Ivan ended that tradition. Thousands of Novgorod's leading families were exiled or killed. This showed that resistance to Moscow would be met with force. Ivan III also built alliances abroad, including marrying Sophia Palaiologina, a relative of the Byzantine imperial family. This marriage gave him a sense of imperial legitimacy.

Breaking the Mongol Yoke

The symbolic breaking of the "Mongol Yoke" is often dated to 1480. At the Ugra River standoff, Ivan III refused to pay further tribute. The Mongol Khan brought an army, but eventually withdrew without a pitched battle. This event is sometimes seen as the moment when Russia became free from Mongol domination. In reality, the influence of the Mongols did not vanish at once, but it was a turning point.

After 1480, Ivan III took the title "Grand Prince of All Rus," emphasizing unity under Moscow's rule. He introduced reforms aimed at centralizing power, reducing the independence of local princes and boyars. While these changes helped create a more cohesive state, they also increased fear among the nobility. Rebellious boyars risked imprisonment, confiscation of lands, or execution. Ivan III understood the value of intimidation, a practice that would grow under his successors.

Early Life of Ivan IV (Ivan the Terrible)

Ivan III's work to strengthen the state continued through his son Vasili III and eventually to his grandson, Ivan IV. Born in 1530, Ivan IV experienced a childhood marked by court intrigue and violence. When Vasili III died, Ivan was only three years old. A regency council, composed of boyars, took over the actual running of the state. Rival clans within the boyar class fought for control, often resorting to murder or the removal of any threats. Ivan saw this struggle up close.

From an early age, Ivan noticed how easily power could shift. He witnessed the mistreatment of his own relatives. Accounts mention that Ivan once complained of being poorly clothed and even half-starved while boyars squabbled over control of the treasury and governance. These experiences shaped his personality. As a young ruler, he grew suspicious, convinced that the boyars were selfish and untrustworthy.

Crowning as the First Tsar

In 1547, at the age of 16, Ivan was crowned as "Tsar of All Rus." This title had never been used by a Russian ruler before. While previous rulers called themselves "Grand Princes," the new title of "Tsar" drew from the word "Caesar," aiming to place the Russian monarch on par with European kings and even the Byzantine emperors. This formal shift in title revealed Ivan's ambition. It also signaled a new era in which the Russian ruler sought to hold absolute power.

Early in his reign, Ivan IV showed promise as a reformer. He worked with a council of advisors known as the "Chosen Council." They introduced changes to the military, the church, and local governance. Some peasants found it easier to bring complaints against corrupt officials, and certain legal procedures were standardized. However, these efforts at reform coexisted with Ivan's growing paranoia and harsh tactics. The story of Ivan IV is one of a ruler who began with some positive changes but ended up remembered primarily for terror.

The Kazan Campaigns and the Expansion of Russia

One of Ivan IV's notable successes was the conquest of the Tatar Khanates of Kazan and Astrakhan. These were remnants of the Mongol Empire. Kazan, located along the Volga River, posed a constant military threat. By seizing Kazan in 1552, Ivan gained control over a significant trade route. This victory also paved the way for Russia's expansion into the Volga region and further east.

The campaign against Kazan was bloody. The siege of the city involved heavy artillery bombardment. When Russian forces breached the walls, they showed little mercy. Many Tatar defenders and civilians were killed, and survivors were taken captive. Ivan ordered the construction of a cathedral in Moscow, St. Basil's Cathedral, to commemorate this triumph. Tourists today admire its colorful domes, not always aware that it was built to mark a brutal conquest.

With Kazan subdued, Ivan's armies moved against the Khanate of Astrakhan near the Caspian Sea. Once that, too, was brought under Moscow's rule, trade routes opened up for Russian merchants. These conquests boosted Ivan's reputation as a ruler who could protect and expand his realm. But war also cost a great deal, both in terms of resources and manpower. To pay for these campaigns, Ivan relied on heavy taxes. Peasants felt the weight of these demands. In some cases, entire villages struggled to meet tax obligations, leading to hunger and flight.

The Birth of the Oprichnina

Ivan IV's reign took a darker turn in the 1560s. His beloved wife, Anastasia Romanovna, died in 1560. Ivan believed she was poisoned, blaming the boyars for the tragedy. Around the same time, Russia became embroiled in the Livonian War (1558–1583) against various European powers, including Sweden and Poland-Lithuania. The war went poorly, draining the state's treasury and morale. These stresses deepened Ivan's suspicion of internal betrayal.

In 1565, Ivan created the Oprichnina, a separate administrative zone under his direct control. He handpicked a force known as the oprichniki to police this territory. Clad in black robes and riding black horses, the oprichniki were infamous for their cruelty. They carried dog heads and broom symbols, signifying their role in sniffing out treason and sweeping away Ivan's enemies. The entire system aimed to crush the power of the boyars, ensuring that only Ivan held supreme authority.

Terrorizing the Boyars

Under the Oprichnina, the tsar claimed large portions of land for himself, forcibly relocating nobles who lived there. The oprichniki would arrive unannounced, confiscate estates, and sometimes execute the owners on charges of treason. Families were torn apart, and boyars found themselves powerless against accusations. Even minor slights could lead to torture or death. Fear spread like wildfire among the nobility, who had no way to defend themselves.

Ivan also used the Oprichnina to punish entire towns. The most infamous example occurred in 1570, when Ivan suspected the city of Novgorod of conspiring against him with Lithuania. The oprichniki descended on Novgorod, looting homes, torturing residents, and burning buildings. Thousands died in what can be seen as a form of state terror. The city, once a center of trade and culture, never fully recovered.

The Oprichnina lasted until 1572, when Ivan abruptly disbanded it. By that time, the damage was done. The boyar class had been severely weakened, and a sense of dread filled the land. Yet, ironically, the system did little to boost Russia's fortunes in the Livonian War. Heavy-handed domestic policies did not translate into success on the battlefield. Many skilled military leaders had been executed or lived in fear.

Effects on the Common People

While much of the Oprichnina's brutality targeted the nobility, ordinary people also suffered. The oprichniki could demand food, shelter, or anything else they wanted. Resistance meant swift punishment. Taxes rose to fund the war and the Oprichnina apparatus. When peasants could not pay, they risked beatings, enslavement, or forced relocation. Some fled to frontier regions, seeking freedom from oppression. These refugees sometimes joined Cossack communities, which became havens for runaway serfs and others escaping harsh control.

The wars and political purges disrupted agricultural production. Famines became more frequent. In some regions, livestock and grain were taken for the army, leaving peasants to starve. Scenes of despair grew common, with entire villages abandoned or falling into ruin. Stories of torture, mass executions, and forced labor circulated widely, ensuring that Ivan's rule was associated with terror. Despite the centralization of power, the price paid by the population was immense.

Legacy of Ivan the Terrible

Ivan IV died in 1584, leaving behind a complicated legacy. On one hand, he had significantly expanded Russia's territory, conquered the Tatar khanates, and made the title of tsar a fixture in Russian politics. The state became more centralized, and the Orthodox Church supported Ivan's rule, seeing him as a protector against foreign powers. On the other hand, his reign unleashed unprecedented violence against the nobility and commoners alike. The Oprichnina created a model for a fear-based approach to ruling, where loyalty was secured through the threat of punishment.

Ivan's personal life was also tragic. He reportedly killed his own son, Ivan Ivanovich, in a fit of rage in 1581. This event left the succession in uncertainty, as his only remaining heir was the weak and possibly mentally challenged Fyodor. Many historians see this as a major factor that contributed to the Time of Troubles—an era of chaos, famine, and civil war that followed Ivan's death.

Setting the Stage for Turmoil

With no strong heir, the line of succession became confused after Ivan's passing. Boyars and other power-hungry figures saw an opportunity to influence or control the throne. Social order had already been weakened by years of violence and high taxes. The wars had drained the treasury. The possibility of foreign intervention grew, as neighboring states recognized Russia's internal problems.

In the midst of this precarious situation, the seeds of a national crisis were planted. The Time of Troubles, which will be the focus of the next chapter, showed just how fragile the Russian state could be, despite Ivan's efforts at centralization. His reign ended with a population traumatized by terror. The methods he used to break the boyars and unify the land had also created profound resentment and instability.

Conclusion

The rise of Muscovy from a small principality under Mongol domination to a major power in Eastern Europe was a long and complex process. Clever alliances, strategic tax collection, and relentless military expansion helped Moscow overshadow its rivals. The achievements of Ivan III and his successors cemented Moscow's role as the nucleus of a unified Russian state. Yet these achievements did not come without cost. Conflict, forced tribute, and subjugation of cities like Novgorod left deep wounds.

Ivan IV, crowned the first Tsar of All Rus, exemplified both the achievements and horrors of this new order. He pushed Russia's borders outward and reformed aspects of its administration. At the same time, he unleashed the Oprichnina, a reign of terror that claimed the lives and livelihoods of many nobles and commoners. His paranoia and cruelty became legendary, and he left a kingdom on the brink of disaster. The stories of torture chambers, mass executions, and forced relocations still alarm those who study his reign. Even though Russia emerged from the 16th century with greater territory and centralized power, it was also burdened by fear, suspicion, and the seeds of future crisis.

The next chapter will reveal how the instability after Ivan the Terrible's death led Russia into one of the most chaotic and frightening periods in its history: the Time of Troubles. In that era, famine, pretenders to the throne, and foreign interventions combined to create a nightmare for ordinary people. The violence seen under Ivan IV did not simply vanish with his death—it set a precedent that would echo in the struggles to come.

CHAPTER 4

THE TIME OF TROUBLES AND FALSE TSARS

Introduction

Ivan the Terrible's reign ended in 1584. Although he had expanded Russia's borders and centralized certain parts of the state, his legacy of violence and instability set the stage for a disastrous period. This era, from the late 1590s into the early 17th century, is known as the Time of Troubles. It was characterized by famine, social unrest, constant power struggles, and the appearance of multiple impostors claiming to be legitimate heirs to the throne—often called False Dmitrys.

During this time, Russia nearly collapsed. Nobles (boyars) fought among themselves, peasants revolted, and foreign powers intervened. One false tsar would rise and then be replaced by another. Neighboring states like Poland-Lithuania saw an opportunity to seize territory. Sweden became involved as well, forging alliances with different Russian factions. Ordinary people suffered the most, trapped between warring groups and devastated by natural disasters that ruined harvests. The Time of Troubles tested the very survival of the Russian state and revealed how quickly fear and chaos could consume a nation weakened by poor leadership and mistrust.

In this chapter, we will look at what led to this crisis, how the false tsars appeared and gained power, and how the chaos engulfed towns and villages. We will also examine the brutal tactics employed by all sides to hold on to power, from the cruelty of invading armies to the merciless actions of Russian nobles trying to maintain control. Finally, we will see how a new dynasty, the Romanovs, emerged from the ashes. But before peace was restored, many horrifying events scarred the land and its people, leaving dark memories that would influence Russia's future.

The Weak Reign of Fyodor I and the Rise of Boris Godunov

When Ivan IV died, his chosen heir was his son Fyodor. But Fyodor was not strong in body or mind; he was often described as pious and gentle but incapable of governing on his own. Real power fell into the hands of Fyodor's brother-in-law, Boris Godunov. Boris had served Ivan the Terrible and gained considerable influence during that time. After Ivan's death, Boris ruled as a de facto regent, guiding state affairs while Fyodor held the title of tsar.

Boris Godunov's Ascendancy

Boris Godunov was a skilled politician. He worked hard to keep the nobility in check, promoted the Russian Orthodox Church, and attempted to maintain stability. Some saw him as a reform-minded figure who tried to ease the burdens on peasants. For instance, he briefly allowed peasants a chance to move to new masters, ending a policy known as "Yuri's Day" restrictions. However, these measures were not enough to prevent an eventual crisis.

When Fyodor died childless in 1598, the Rurik dynasty—descendants of the line that had ruled since the time of Kievan Rus—came to an end. Boris Godunov managed to secure the throne for himself, becoming the first non-Rurik tsar. Initially, his rule seemed promising, but fate would soon deal him a difficult hand.

The Great Famine of 1601–1603

Not long after Boris took power, the climate in Russia went through dramatic changes. There were extremely cold summers and early frosts, destroying crops. Harvests failed. People starved. In some regions, entire villages were depopulated. Bodies piled up in the streets of Moscow. Accounts describe desperate peasants eating grass, bark, or even resorting to cannibalism. The government attempted relief efforts, such as distributing grain from state granaries, but these were inadequate compared to the vast need.

The famine bred discontent. Boris Godunov's opponents whispered that the famine was a sign of God's anger at Boris for seizing the throne. Rumors spread that the rightful heir to the throne had been killed on Boris's orders. These whispers became louder when news surfaced that a man claiming to be Dmitry, Ivan the Terrible's long-lost son, had appeared in Poland-Lithuania.

The First False Dmitry

Ivan IV had a son named Dmitry, who died under mysterious circumstances in 1591 at the town of Uglich. Officially, it was reported that the young prince had died in an accident, possibly stabbing himself with a knife during an epileptic seizure. However, some believed that Boris Godunov had ordered Dmitry murdered to clear the path to the throne. This accusation would haunt Boris for the rest of his life, even if the true circumstances remain unclear.

Appearance of the Pretender

Around 1603, a man emerged in Poland claiming to be Prince Dmitry, who had supposedly survived an assassination attempt. Known to history as the First False Dmitry, he attracted support from Polish nobles and the Jesuits, who saw an opportunity to place a pro-Polish, Catholic-friendly ruler on the Russian throne. He also found backing among some Russian boyars who hated Boris Godunov and saw the pretender as a way to overthrow him.

In 1604, this false Dmitry invaded Russia with a small army. Because of the famine and general discontent, many locals welcomed him or at least did not resist. His supporters claimed he would bring justice and punish Boris for crimes against the true heir. As the pretender marched toward Moscow, Boris Godunov's forces tried to stop him. Initially, Boris's armies held an advantage, but the situation changed dramatically when Boris died suddenly in April 1605.

Taking the Throne

With Boris's death, the people of Moscow revolted against his son, Fyodor Borisovich, who briefly succeeded him. The boyars switched sides, arresting or killing Godunov supporters. The First False Dmitry entered Moscow triumphantly in June 1605. He was crowned tsar, and many at court pretended to believe he was indeed the son of Ivan the Terrible.

Yet, his rule did not last. Nobles who had aided his rise soon feared his growing power. The new tsar tried to introduce certain reforms and moved toward Western ideas, favoring the Polish advisers who had helped him. The Russian Orthodox Church and the traditional boyars grew uneasy. Rumors spread that he planned to convert Russia to Catholicism. Less than a year into his reign, in May 1606, a group of boyars led by Prince Vasili Shuisky stormed the Kremlin. The false Dmitry was killed. His body was displayed to the public, and the boyars declared that he was indeed an impostor sent by the devil.

Reign of Vasili Shuisky and Widening Chaos

Following the assassination of the First False Dmitry, Prince Vasili Shuisky declared himself tsar. However, his hold on power was shaky. Many regions did not acknowledge him as legitimate. Peasant uprisings flared, some led by figures claiming to avenge the murdered "Tsar Dmitry." War-torn lands, famine, and ongoing nobility feuds made Shuisky's position nearly impossible. To make matters worse, new pretenders soon emerged, each claiming to be Dmitry once again.

The Second False Dmitry

In 1607, another man calling himself Dmitry appeared, quickly gaining the nickname of the "Second False Dmitry." Although he never gained control of Moscow, he gathered a sizeable army. This force included peasants who saw him as a potential savior, Polish mercenaries hoping for rewards, and Cossacks who despised the rigid feudal system under the boyars. Shuisky's regime could not defeat this coalition decisively.

At the same time, various factions fought each other. Some boyars supported Shuisky; others backed the false Dmitry. Cossack rebels attacked towns and estates, robbing the wealthy and freeing serfs. Foreign powers saw an opportunity to seize land or influence. Polish troops entered the country under the banner of supporting their "rightful" tsar, while the Swedes allied with Shuisky, hoping to counter Polish moves. The country descended into near-anarchy.

The Siege of Smolensk and Foreign Intervention

One of the most critical points of foreign involvement was the Polish siege of Smolensk (1609–1611). King Sigismund III of Poland aimed to place his son, Władysław, on the Russian throne. Polish forces attacked the fortress city of Smolensk. The siege lasted for months, leading to tremendous suffering for the defenders. Starvation, disease, and constant bombardment tore the city apart. When Smolensk finally fell in 1611, the road to Moscow lay open for Polish troops.

The Poles then advanced on Moscow, where they occupied the Kremlin in 1610. Tsar Vasili Shuisky had already been deposed by boyars who sought to negotiate with the Polish king. A Polish garrison settled into the capital, controlling the seat of power. Some Russian nobles even entertained the idea of placing King Sigismund's son on the throne, hoping to end the chaos. However, many Russians, including the church leadership, viewed this as a betrayal. Anti-Polish sentiment grew among both nobles and commoners.

Resistance and the Rise of National Forces

Despite the occupation, large parts of Russia did not accept Polish rule. The Orthodox Church called on Russians to drive out the foreign invaders and false tsars. Merchant leaders in cities like Nizhny Novgorod took up arms, forming militias. In 1611 and 1612, two major volunteer armies assembled. The second army, led by Kuzma Minin (a merchant) and Prince Dmitry Pozharsky (a noble), managed to rally people from different classes. They marched on Moscow in 1612.

In a series of battles around the capital, these volunteers forced the Polish garrison to retreat into the Kremlin. Cut off from supplies, the Poles eventually surrendered. This moment is considered a turning point, showing that Russians could unite against a common enemy despite internal differences. The success of Minin and Pozharsky laid the groundwork for a new government.

Horror Stories from the Time of Troubles

While grand political and military actions were taking place, ordinary Russians faced terror on a daily basis. Armies, whether loyal to Shuisky, a false tsar, or a foreign king, often looted towns and villages. They stole food, burned homes, and assaulted local people. Peasants were forced to give up their last stores of grain to feed whichever army controlled their region at the time. If they refused, the soldiers might execute entire families. Disease spread as the normal rhythms of farming and trade collapsed. Starvation claimed thousands of lives.

In some cases, entire towns pledged loyalty to one pretender, only to be punished by another. Stories tell of mass executions in public squares, of boyars turning on each other in savage ways. Private armies roamed the countryside, kidnapping peasants for ransom or forcing them into military service. Families were split apart. Many who escaped violent death fell victim to hunger or plague. Despair was rampant, and the constant shift in power made life unpredictable.

The Plight of Serfs and Cossacks

Serfs found themselves in an even more desperate position. Some saw the chaos as a chance to break free from the feudal system. They joined Cossack bands or rebel forces, looting noble estates. Others were forced to remain on the land, trapped by local lords who demanded loyalty. The distinction between "official" and "rebel" blurred, since each faction claimed legitimacy. For many serfs, it was simply a struggle to stay alive.

Cossacks, traditionally living on the frontiers, also had mixed roles. Some sided with the Polish or the false tsars to gain wealth. Others aimed to protect their independence from Moscow or any centralized power. As a result, different Cossack groups fought each other. Their raids added yet another layer of fear for the general population. In the power vacuum of the Time of Troubles, anyone with weapons and a small following could impose terror on local communities.

The Emergence of the Romanovs

By late 1612, the Polish forces in Moscow were defeated, and the city was liberated. Yet the country still lacked a clear ruler. The Zemsky Sobor (an assembly of representatives from different social groups, including nobles, clergy, and merchants) convened to choose a new tsar. In 1613, they elected Mikhail Romanov, a 16-year-old boy from a family related to Ivan IV's first wife, Anastasia. This marked the beginning of the Romanov dynasty, which would rule Russia for the next 300 years.

Hope and Relief

Mikhail Romanov's election provided a moment of unity. Many Russians, exhausted by years of war and famine, accepted him as the rightful ruler. The boyars hoped he would be easier to control, while the common people prayed that a new dynasty would bring peace. Under Mikhail's early reign, efforts were made to stabilize the country. Negotiations with Sweden and Poland led to peace treaties, though Russia lost some territories. Internal reforms began slowly, as the young tsar and his advisors tried to rebuild a shattered realm.

Still, it took many years to recover from the devastation. Entire regions lay desolate. Farm fields had grown wild, and many skilled workers had fled or died. Famine and disease did not disappear overnight. The new government also had to deal with leftover rebel groups and Cossacks who refused to lay down arms. But at least there was a recognized monarch, which helped restore a basic structure to governance.

Lasting Consequences

The Time of Troubles left deep scars on Russian society. The death toll from famine, plague, and warfare was enormous. Towns and villages that had once been centers of trade were destroyed or seriously weakened. The economy was in shambles. People who survived carried the memory of terror, betrayal, and violence. These events taught a harsh lesson about how quickly a kingdom could dissolve when leadership was weak and unity was lost.

Strengthening the Autocracy

One of the significant outcomes of the Time of Troubles was the eventual strengthening of the autocracy. The boyars had shown themselves to be divided and easily swayed by personal gain. Foreign interventions had proven that Russia needed a strong central ruler to defend its borders. The Orthodox Church also played a role in supporting a powerful tsar, seeing the monarch as a defender of the faith.

Over time, the Romanovs would further centralize power, continuing and expanding the system of serfdom. They believed that a tightly controlled and disciplined society was necessary to prevent another breakdown like the Time of Troubles. This push toward stronger autocratic rule also served the interests of the nobility who had survived, as they cooperated with the throne in return for privileges and control over the peasantry.

Impact on the Russian Psyche

Beyond the political ramifications, the Time of Troubles had a profound effect on the mindset of many Russians. Tales of the false Dmitrys, the brutal occupation of Moscow by foreign troops, and the mass starvation became part of folklore. Even church writings emphasized these calamities as a punishment for moral failings, urging people to remain loyal to the rightful ruler. Fear of foreign invasion and internal division lingered.

This history reinforced the idea that chaos would erupt if power fragmented. Many believed that only a strong hand at the top could keep the country from falling apart. Over the centuries, future rulers often invoked the memory of the Time of Troubles to justify harsh measures. They argued that strong autocratic rule was the only way to protect Russia from internal and external threats.

CHAPTER 5

THE EARLY ROMANOVS AND THE HARSH LIFE OF SERFS

Introduction

The Time of Troubles ended in 1613 with the crowning of Mikhail Romanov, a young man from a boyar family related to Ivan the Terrible's first wife. Although the new tsar was just 16 years old, he and his advisors took on the massive task of rebuilding a shattered country. Famine, foreign occupation, and social unrest had left deep wounds. Many towns lay in ruins, and the population had plummeted due to starvation, disease, and warfare.

Mikhail Romanov's election was a signal of hope. People hoped for an end to chaos and the start of stability. Over the following decades, the Romanov dynasty worked to restore order by strengthening central authority and forging alliances with powerful nobles (boyars). While this consolidation did bring some measure of peace, it also had a dark side: the tightening grip of serfdom.

Serfdom had existed in various forms in Russia long before the Romanovs, but it became far more rigid and oppressive under their rule. This chapter explores the early Romanov rulers—Mikhail, his son Alexis, and successors—while focusing on the harsh realities faced by serfs. Bound to the land, forced to labor for their landlords, and subjected to brutal punishments, these peasants formed the bulk of Russia's population. Their suffering was a key feature of the Romanov era, shaping Russia's social and economic structure for centuries.

The Reign of Mikhail Romanov (1613–1645)

Rebuilding a Ravaged Land

When Mikhail Romanov was chosen by the Zemsky Sobor (the assembly of the land), one of his first tasks was simply to restore governance. Many local officials had fled or been killed during the Time of Troubles. Law and order broke down in many regions, where marauders and bandits roamed unchecked. Mikhail relied heavily on his father, Filaret, who returned from captivity and became Patriarch of the Russian Orthodox Church. Together, they formed a strong alliance between the throne and the church, promoting the idea that the tsar ruled by divine right.

Mikhail's government began negotiating peace treaties with neighboring states. Treaties with Sweden and the Polish-Lithuanian Commonwealth brought a measure of stability, although Russia had to concede some territories. The urgent priority was to bring the countryside back under control. That meant dealing with Cossacks, roaming soldiers, and groups of peasants who had taken up arms or fled their lands during the chaos.

To encourage nobles to support the new regime, Mikhail confirmed their rights to the land. This confirmation often came with an unstated promise to help them retrieve runaway serfs. As a result, one of the early policies was reinforcing rules that tied peasants more firmly to the estates where they worked. In exchange, the boyars pledged loyalty to the young tsar, helping to rebuild an army and restore basic administration.

Financial Struggles and Taxation

The treasury was nearly empty after years of war and disorder. The state needed funds for everything—reconstructing fortresses, maintaining a small standing army, and paying officials. The government thus expanded taxes on common people. Salt taxes, grain taxes, and other levies increased. For wealthy merchants or boyars, these taxes were burdensome but not ruinous. For peasants, however, higher taxes added to an already heavy load.

Many peasants could barely produce enough grain to feed their families, let alone pay new taxes. Those who failed to pay faced severe punishments, including beatings, fines, or forced labor. Sometimes entire villages were raided by tax collectors accompanied by armed guards. If a village was declared in arrears, the authorities might seize livestock or crops, leaving the peasants with nothing. Such harsh measures caused resentment and further bound peasants to their landlords, as they had few other means of survival.

Codifying Serfdom: The Legal Framework

Over the decades following the Time of Troubles, laws were introduced and refined to tie peasants permanently to the land. This was not a sudden process but a series of changes that gradually reduced peasant freedoms. One of the most important legal milestones came in 1649 under Tsar Alexis, Mikhail's son. However, the groundwork for that transformation began under Mikhail himself.

Restricted Movement

For centuries, peasants had some limited rights to move from one landlord to another, especially around the time of Yuri's Day (a specific date in late autumn). But by the early 17th century, these rights were being curtailed more and more, especially if peasants had unpaid debts or taxes. The turmoil of the Time of Troubles had seen huge numbers of peasants fleeing their homes to escape war, famine, or oppressive masters. Landlords complained that they had lost their workforce. To appease these landlords, the state issued decrees limiting peasant movement.

Under Mikhail, the government increased the statute of limitations for catching runaway peasants. If a peasant escaped a cruel landlord, that landlord could now pursue them over many years, dragging them back to face severe penalties. This bolstered the landowners' power and discouraged peasants from leaving, even under brutal conditions.

Church Support

The Orthodox Church generally supported stricter laws on peasants. Many in the church leadership believed social order was best maintained when people stayed in their ordained place. Church sermons emphasized obedience to the tsar and the landlords. Some priests tried to protect peasants from overly cruel masters, but the institution as a whole did not oppose the tightening of serfdom. Landowning monasteries and bishoprics also depended on peasant labor, so they had a vested interest in limiting peasant mobility.

Life Under Serfdom

For peasants, the daily reality of serfdom was marked by hard labor, limited autonomy, and the threat of brutal punishment. The master of the estate—whether a noble, a member of the royal family, or the church—claimed not just the right to a peasant's labor, but also significant control over personal matters.

Daily Toil

A typical serf day started before sunrise. Men plowed fields, tended to livestock, or performed specialized tasks like blacksmithing if required. Women prepared meals, wove cloth, took care of household chores, and often joined men in fieldwork during critical seasons like planting or harvesting. Children were expected to help from a young age, herding animals or gathering wood. Rest periods were rare, mostly limited to religious holidays.

Landlords demanded a portion of the harvest, along with additional obligations called "barshchina" (labor owed to the lord's own fields) or "obrok" (a payment in goods or money). Some peasants had to work three or more days per week on the lord's fields, using their own tools and livestock. This left them little time to tend their own small plots, making hunger a constant threat.

Punishments and Controls

Serfdom was maintained through a network of fear. Landlords or their overseers could administer punishment for disobedience, laziness, or minor offenses. This might take the form of beatings with rods or whips. Chronic offenders could face harsher penalties, like branding or even being sold to a distant estate. While technically peasants were not "slaves" who could be sold without land, in practice, many landlords found ways to separate peasants from their home plots and send them elsewhere.

Stories spread of sadistic landlords who tormented serfs for amusement or personal grudges. While such extreme cruelty was not universal, the threat always loomed. Legal recourse for peasants was minimal. A peasant could, in theory, complain to local officials or the landlord's superiors, but more often than not, these complaints were ignored or led to further retaliation. Fear and powerlessness kept most peasants in line.

Tsar Alexis (1645–1676) and the Ulozhenie of 1649

When Mikhail Romanov died in 1645, his son Alexis took the throne. Only 16 years old at his coronation, Alexis nonetheless grew into a forceful ruler. Known as a devout Orthodox Christian, he placed great emphasis on upholding traditional order. Under his reign, Russia fought wars with Poland, dealt with internal revolts, and underwent important religious reforms that caused a schism in the church. But perhaps his most lasting impact was the new legal code known as the Sobornoye Ulozhenie of 1649.

The Sobornoye Ulozhenie

This comprehensive legal code was meant to unify and update Russia's many laws, some of which dated back to medieval times. It had sections on criminal law, property rights, and government administration. Notably, it included strict provisions on serfs and runaway peasants:

1. **Abolition of the Statute of Limitations on Runaways**: Before this, landlords had a set number of years to find and reclaim escaped peasants. The new code removed any time limit. A peasant who fled even decades ago could be dragged back.
2. **Harsh Penalties for Helpers**: Anyone found aiding or hiding runaway peasants faced severe punishment, including heavy fines or corporal punishment.
3. **Strengthening Landlord Authority**: Landlords gained more power to police their estates and punish peasants. Local officials were required to assist in returning runaways, further embedding the idea that peasants were under a master's control.

Social Unrest and Revolts

The tightening grip on serfs fueled anger, especially among those who saw no escape from exploitation. In some towns, merchants and lower-class citizens also faced new taxes and restrictions. Riots broke out in cities like Moscow over issues like salt taxes or rising prices. Cossack uprisings on the southern frontiers merged with peasant revolts, forming major rebellions. The most famous of these was led by Stenka Razin in the 1660s, where Cossacks and peasants captured cities along the Volga River. They proclaimed freedom from oppression and threatened to march on Moscow.

Tsar Alexis responded with brutal force. Rebel towns were retaken, and leaders were executed publicly. Still, the government did make some minor reforms to ease tensions, but there was no rollback of serfdom. Instead, the state concluded that a firm hand was needed to maintain order. More soldiers were stationed in key areas, and the church reinforced obedience to the tsar as a religious duty.

Church Schism and Its Impact on Serfs

During Alexis's reign, Patriarch Nikon tried to reform certain church rituals to align them more closely with the Greek Orthodox tradition. These changes included revising prayer books and making the sign of the cross with three fingers instead of two. Many Russians saw these seemingly small alterations as heresy. Those who resisted came to be called Old Believers.

Persecution of the Old Believers

Tsar Alexis sided with Patriarch Nikon initially and punished Old Believers who refused to adopt the new practices. Some were exiled, imprisoned, or executed for what was deemed religious rebellion. Entire communities of peasants and small towns that followed the Old Believer tradition faced harassment from state authorities. This added another layer of oppression, especially in regions where the Old Belief was strong.

Some Old Believers fled to remote areas in the north or east, establishing isolated settlements. Here, peasants tried to live outside the state's reach, hoping to escape forced labor and religious persecution. The government labeled many of these communities as illegal, sending soldiers to destroy them if they became too large or defiant. Thus, religious conflict intersected with the broader issues of serfdom, as both the church and the state demanded strict obedience.

Tsar Fyodor III and Continuing Pressures

When Alexis died in 1676, his son Fyodor III inherited the throne. Although he reigned only until 1682, Fyodor attempted to modernize certain aspects of governance, including reforming the military and abolishing some outdated ranks in the nobility. However, the question of serfdom remained largely untouched. The system had become deeply woven into Russia's economic and social fabric. Landowners relied on forced labor to produce surplus goods, while the state relied on these same landowners for tax revenue and military support.

Under Fyodor, the legal framework for serfdom stayed in place. Tax burdens did not ease much for peasants. Local officials continued to enforce discipline with harsh methods, ensuring that peasants complied with their obligations. Although less famous than his father or successors, Fyodor presided over a Russia where the gap between nobles and peasants kept growing.

Some minor improvements in administration and attempts to curb corruption did occur under Fyodor, but none of these initiatives significantly changed the plight of the serfs. The seeds were planted for future unrest, though the massive changes that would come under Peter the Great overshadowed Fyodor's short reign.

The Human Cost: Stories of Despair and Resistance

While official records focus on laws, taxes, and decrees, the human side of serfdom was often grim. Travelers from Western Europe who visited Russia during this period left accounts of peasants living in what they described as near-slavery. They saw wretched huts, malnourished families, and severe punishments. These reports varied in accuracy, but they do highlight the shock that many foreigners felt when witnessing Russian serfdom up close.

Family Separations

Serfs were technically bound to the land, meaning they were not to be sold off separately from the estate. But in practice, landlords sometimes found ways around this rule. They would partition lands and sell them to relatives or business partners, splitting families in the process. Children might end up on a neighboring estate while parents remained behind. The heartbreak of separation was devastating, and there was no legal system to protect family unity.

Forced Labor on State Projects

At times, the state demanded corvée labor (unpaid labor for the government) from serfs and townspeople alike. Large-scale construction projects—like building fortresses or roads—relied on coerced labor. Peasants found themselves transported hundreds of miles from home for months, working under harsh conditions. Many died from exposure, poor nutrition, or accidents on these sites. No compensation awaited their families if they perished.

Escapes and Frontier Life

Despite the high risk, some serfs chose to flee. The southern steppes and eastern regions offered relative freedom if one could evade capture. This was part of how the Cossack communities in places like the Don River basin or Siberia grew. Runaway serfs formed new settlements beyond the state's immediate reach. Some joined bands of raiders, attacking merchant caravans or even government convoys. While these runaways lived dangerously, they preferred uncertainty to the guaranteed oppression at home.

Landowners constantly pressured the government to crack down on runaways. Raids into frontier areas sometimes brought fugitives back in chains. Yet, the vastness of Russia made total control impossible. The dream of escape lingered, feeding into larger rebellions whenever a charismatic leader emerged to promise freedom from serfdom.

CHAPTER 6

PETER THE GREAT'S REFORMS AND METHODS OF CONTROL

Introduction

By the late 17th century, Russia was still very much a traditional society with a rigid social hierarchy. The Romanov dynasty had weathered early turmoil, tightened serfdom, and maintained alliances with powerful boyars. However, the world was changing. Western Europe experienced scientific discoveries, maritime expansion, and the growth of strong centralized states. When Peter I (commonly known as Peter the Great) came to power, he brought an intense desire to modernize Russia, catch up with Europe's military might, and transform cultural norms.

Peter embarked on a massive program of reforms, from reorganizing the army to introducing new administrative structures. He also forced a cultural revolution, demanding that nobles shave their beards and adopt Western dress. He founded the city of St. Petersburg in a swampy area near the Baltic Sea, forcibly relocating thousands of workers to build it. While Peter's efforts did modernize Russia's military and bureaucracy, they also unleashed suffering on ordinary people. His projects required huge resources and labor, often obtained through coercion. The state developed new means of control, expanding the power of the tsar at the expense of the nobility and the church.

In this chapter, we will explore Peter the Great's rise to power, his key reforms, and the harsh methods he used to ensure compliance. We will look at the cost paid by peasants, soldiers, and even his own family members. While Peter is remembered as a visionary who propelled Russia onto the European stage, he is also known for his ruthless tactics, public executions, and fear-based governance. His rule offers a stark example of how modernization from above can come with a high human price.

Early Life and Ascension to the Throne

Peter was born in 1672, the son of Tsar Alexei Mikhailovich and his second wife, Natalya Naryshkina. His half-brother, Fyodor III, ruled briefly before dying without a male heir. Another half-brother, Ivan V, was weak in both mind and body, yet he was older than Peter. A power struggle within the royal family allowed Peter and Ivan to share the throne as co-tsars, though the real power was initially held by Peter's half-sister, Sophia, who acted as regent.

Streltsy Revolt

In 1682, a group of palace guards known as the Streltsy revolted, influenced partly by boyars who backed Sophia's regency. The uprising resulted in brutal violence at the Kremlin. Several of Peter's relatives and supporters were killed in front of his eyes. This traumatic event stayed with Peter, fueling his distrust of the old military units and the traditional nobility. Eventually, Peter removed Sophia from power, sending her to a convent. He assumed more control, although he still officially shared the throne with Ivan V until Ivan's death in 1696.

These early experiences shaped Peter's ruling style. He saw disloyalty and conspiracies lurking everywhere, and he resolved to build a new military system that would be loyal only to him. He also recognized the need to modernize Russia's armed forces if it was to compete with European powers like Sweden and the Ottoman Empire.

Peter's Grand Embassy and Western Influences

One of Peter's defining moments came with his famous "Grand Embassy" to Western Europe in 1697–1698. He traveled incognito, though most people knew who he was, to learn about shipbuilding, navigation, and modern technology. He visited shipyards in the Dutch Republic and England, studied military tactics, and recruited foreign experts to come to Russia. This journey fueled his ambition to create a modern navy and reorganize the army along European lines.

Return and Crackdown

Peter cut his trip short in 1698 when he received word of another Streltsy uprising in Moscow. Upon returning, he punished the rebels severely. Thousands were executed or flogged. Public hangings were meant to send a clear message that no one should challenge the tsar's authority. Peter personally took part in some of the interrogations, underscoring his hands-on approach to discipline. The brutality of the crackdown showed how far he was willing to go to secure his reign.

Military Reforms and the Great Northern War

Armed with knowledge from Western Europe, Peter reorganized the Russian army and navy. He introduced modern drills, new forms of artillery, and a European-style ranking system. He established the Table of Ranks later in his reign, which allowed talented individuals (even from non-noble backgrounds) to rise through the military or civil service based on merit. This was revolutionary for a society so steeped in hereditary privileges.

The Great Northern War (1700–1721)

Peter's biggest test came with the Great Northern War against Sweden. At the time, Sweden was a major military power, controlling territories along the Baltic Sea. Peter aimed to seize these lands, giving Russia access to warm-water ports for trade. Early in the war, Russia suffered a disastrous defeat at the Battle of Narva in 1700. But Peter learned from this failure, improved his army, and slowly pushed back the Swedes over the next two decades.

The war was long, brutal, and costly. Peter imposed new taxes to fund his military campaigns. He conscripted peasants into the army for life, ripping them away from their families. Entire regions were taxed heavily to support the building of warships. On the battlefield, Russian soldiers experienced harsh discipline. Desertion was punishable by death, and officers were known to treat common soldiers with extreme severity. Yet, by the war's end in 1721, Russia emerged victorious, gaining significant territories along the Baltic coast.

Building St. Petersburg: A Monument to Ambition

One of Peter's most famous projects was the construction of a new capital city: St. Petersburg. He chose a marshy, mosquito-infested area near the Neva River. Despite its inhospitable climate, he believed this location would give Russia a "window to Europe," facilitating trade and diplomacy. The decision to build a grand city in this swamp showed both Peter's determination and his disregard for human costs.

Forced Labor and High Mortality

Tens of thousands of peasants, soldiers, and convicts were conscripted to work on the city's foundations. They drained swamps, drove wooden piles into the mud, and hauled heavy stones for fortress walls. Conditions were miserable. Workers lived in crude huts or slept in the open. Disease ran rampant, with malaria and dysentery claiming countless lives. The death toll was so high that Russians later called the city "built on bones."

Yet Peter pushed forward. He threatened severe punishments for anyone who tried to flee. Nobles were ordered to build palaces in the new city and relocate there. Foreign architects and engineers were brought in to design European-style buildings. Over time, the city grew into a striking symbol of Russia's new ambitions. But beneath the beautiful facades lay the memory of mass suffering.

Cultural Reforms and Social Control

Peter was not satisfied with just modernizing the military and building a city. He wanted to transform Russian society at its core. He ordered nobles to adopt Western clothing and shave their beards. Those who refused had to pay a special "beard tax." Traditional long robes were replaced by European-style coats. Even the calendar was changed to match Western practice, and the new year was shifted from September 1 to January 1.

The Role of Women

Peter also made changes that affected women in noble families. He encouraged them to attend public events like balls and assemblies, which were modeled after European courts. This was a significant shift in a society where upper-class women were often secluded in separate quarters. While it did open some social opportunities, it was mostly the nobility who benefited. Serf women continued to live in the same harsh conditions as before.

Church Subjugation

Peter saw the Russian Orthodox Church as a potential threat to his reforms, especially because it had long championed traditional values. When Patriarch Adrian died in 1700, Peter refused to name a new patriarch. Instead, he installed a system of church governance called the Holy Synod, led by a lay official appointed by the tsar. This move effectively put the church under state control. Clergy who disagreed were silenced, exiled, or forced to comply. Peter seized church lands and used their revenues for state projects, further tightening his grip on all aspects of Russian life.

Serfs Under Peter's Rule

Peter inherited a society where serfdom was already deeply rooted. Far from improving peasants' lives, his modernization drive often made them even harder. While some historians argue that Peter's reforms eventually spurred economic development, ordinary serfs saw immediate increases in taxes, conscription, and forced labor.

Military Conscription

To fill the ranks of the new model army, Peter instituted a draft that could last a lifetime. Serf families dreaded the arrival of recruiters, knowing they might never see their sons again. Once conscripted, a serf was considered state property, subject to harsh military discipline. The pay was minimal, and desertion meant brutal punishment. Families left behind lost an important source of labor, making it harder to meet the landlord's demands.

Increase in Taxes

Peter introduced new taxes on everything from beehives to household items. The most famous was the "soul tax," a poll tax levied on each male peasant. The landlord often collected it and paid the government, adding fees to cover their own costs. Failure to pay meant punishment or seizure of property. Since serfs were already barely surviving, these added burdens led many deeper into poverty.

Forced Labor for State Projects

Beyond the building of St. Petersburg, Peter demanded labor for canals, roads, and factories. For instance, the state established iron foundries in the Ural Mountains, where serfs and convicts toiled under dangerous conditions. Living quarters were cramped, and accidents were frequent. The region's harsh winters worsened the misery. Though Russia did gain industrial capacity, the human toll was steep.

Brutal Suppression of Dissent

Peter did not tolerate opposition. Anyone suspected of plotting against his reforms or authority faced immediate retaliation. This included not just the old nobility but sometimes even members of Peter's own family. His half-sister, Sophia, had been confined to a convent. Later, he clashed with his son, Tsarevich Alexei, who disagreed with many of his father's policies.

The Tragedy of Tsarevich Alexei

Alexei grew up watching his father's relentless reforms. Some say he disliked Western ways and secretly aligned with conservative factions in the church and nobility. Accused of treason and possibly plotting to flee Russia, Alexei was arrested in 1718. Peter ordered harsh interrogations, and Alexei died in prison—some sources suggest torture or mistreatment was the cause. The event highlighted Peter's readiness to destroy even his blood relations if they stood in the way of his vision.

Public Executions and Displays

Peter made a spectacle of punishing traitors. Executions in public squares were common. Heads of rebels might be left on display for months as a warning. People were forced to watch these events, reinforcing a culture of fear. While intended to deter conspiracies, such cruelty also bred deep resentment among many Russians who felt that the reforms came at too high a moral and human cost.

Peter's Legacy of Modernization and Fear

Peter the Great died in 1725, leaving behind a transformed Russia. Under his leadership, the country emerged as a major European power with a modernized military, an expanding navy, and a new capital city. Diplomatically, Russia became an influential player, recognized by Western states as a force to be reckoned with. He also introduced changes in art, education, and administration that set Russia on a path toward further development in the 18th century.

However, the cost of these changes was enormous. Countless peasants died building St. Petersburg or serving in the military. Taxes and forced labor weighed heavily on the common people. The nobility saw their traditional privileges challenged, but they eventually adapted to the new order and even embraced Western fashions. Many old customs were lost or suppressed, leading to cultural tensions that would surface in later generations.

Influence on Future Rulers

Peter's style of autocratic leadership became a model for subsequent tsars. They inherited a more centralized state apparatus, including a bureaucracy and a standing army. The principle that the tsar's word stood above all remained deeply ingrained. Future rulers like Catherine the Great expanded on Peter's foundation, also using strict measures to maintain power.

Yet for all his achievements, Peter is remembered as much for his ruthlessness as for his vision. His reign showed that modernization can be imposed by force, but the human suffering it causes can leave a deep mark. The image of Russia as a nation that might lurch forward through sweeping reforms, driven by a strong leader, yet at the expense of widespread oppression, took hold under Peter. This dual legacy—progress mixed with cruelty—would color Russian history for centuries.

Conclusion

Peter the Great's reign was a turning point in Russian history. He dragged the country into a new era with vigor, determination, and a willingness to use extreme violence. By the time he died, Russia boasted an empire that stretched from the Baltic to the Pacific, with new institutions modeled on European practices. His drive to build a modern state was successful in many respects, paving the way for more complex trade and diplomatic ties with Europe.

However, the toll on the population—especially serfs—was staggering. They financed Peter's wars and reforms through backbreaking labor, exorbitant taxes, and conscription. Many thousands lost their lives in forced construction projects or on faraway battlefields. Among the nobility and even within his own family, dissent was met with intimidation, torture, and death. Public executions and gruesome displays of punishment helped maintain order in a society being reshaped from the top down.

This chapter highlights the pattern of autocratic power that would persist in Russia: strong rulers implementing rapid changes with minimal regard for human cost. In the chapters to come, we will see how later monarchs, such as Catherine the Great and subsequent Romanovs, built on Peter's reforms while also grappling with peasant unrest, noble plotting, and the shadow of potential revolutions. The push and pull between modernization and control remained a central thread in Russia's story, and the seeds of that struggle were deeply planted during Peter's transformative and terrifying rule.

CHAPTER 7

EMPRESS ELIZABETH, CATHERINE THE GREAT, AND COURT INTRIGUE

Introduction

By the mid-18th century, Russia had already undergone monumental changes under Peter the Great. The state boasted a more modern army, a growing navy, and a new capital city, St. Petersburg. Yet these reforms had come at a great human cost. Serfs and ordinary people continued to toil under heavy burdens, paying for the grand ambitions of the throne. When Peter died, a series of rulers followed, some short-lived and others heavily influenced by powerful courtiers. Eventually, the crown passed to Empress Elizabeth, Peter's daughter, who seized power in a dramatic coup.

Under Elizabeth (reigned 1741–1762), the Russian court became famous for its extravagance and intrigue. Noble families vied for influence, and palace plots abounded. While Elizabeth's reign brought a degree of stability, it did not significantly improve the conditions of the lower classes. Following Elizabeth, power fell into the hands of Catherine the Great, a German princess who married into the Romanov family. She took the throne after another palace coup, removing her husband, Tsar Peter III. Catherine's reign (1762–1796) is often seen as a golden age of the Russian Empire, filled with cultural achievements and territorial expansion. But behind the glitter of her court lay a reality of increased serfdom, harsh control of dissent, and deep divisions between social classes.

In this chapter, we will look at the succession struggles following Peter the Great, highlighting Empress Elizabeth's seizure of power and the lavish court she presided over. We will then move to Catherine the Great, examining her Enlightenment ideals, her quest for expansion, and the dark side of her rule: the strengthening of noble power over serfs and the suppression of those who dared to rebel. Along the way, we will uncover shocking stories of backstabbing, secret alliances, and the harsh realities of life for the common people during one of Russia's most iconic eras.

Empress Elizabeth's Coup and Early Reign

A Dramatic Seizure of Power

After Peter the Great's death in 1725, the Russian throne changed hands multiple times. His second wife, Catherine I, briefly ruled, followed by Peter's grandson, Peter II, and then Empress Anna Ivanovna. When Anna died, a regency took over for the infant Emperor Ivan VI. During this chaotic period, nobles and courtiers maneuvered for power, resulting in shifting alliances and widespread uncertainty about the empire's future direction.

Elizabeth Petrovna, daughter of Peter the Great and Catherine I, had been sidelined during these transitions. However, she was well-liked by the guards regiments in St. Petersburg, partly because she was Peter's direct descendant and partly because of her friendly demeanor. In 1741, Elizabeth staged a sudden coup with the support of these guards. She led soldiers into the Winter Palace, arrested the infant emperor and his regents, and declared herself Empress. This bloodless coup was a stark reminder of how palace guards and high-ranking military units could decide who held the throne.

Promises and Popularity

At first, Elizabeth promised not to execute her political enemies, which earned her some goodwill among nobles and the public. True to her word, she did not order mass executions. Instead, she exiled those who had served the previous regime or posed a threat to her authority. Many were sent to remote parts of the empire, while Ivan VI, the deposed infant emperor, spent the rest of his life in solitary confinement, growing up without freedom or normal human contact.

Elizabeth's popularity soared initially. She was seen as the true heir of Peter the Great, capable of returning Russia to the glory of her father's era. Her court became known for its grand festivities, balls, and splendid ceremonies. Yet, behind these celebrations, the old mechanisms of control stayed in place. Serfs still had no path to freedom. Noble privileges remained protected. The empire's bureaucratic structures and secret police quietly enforced imperial authority.

Elizabeth's Court and Policies

Lavish Lifestyle and Patronage of Arts

One of the hallmarks of Elizabeth's reign was her extravagant lifestyle. She loved fashion, hosting large parties and wearing an endless array of ornate gowns. It is said she never wore the same dress twice. The empress also had a keen interest in music, theater, and architecture. Under her patronage, St. Petersburg saw the construction of new palaces and the development of the arts. The city grew even more magnificent, although the cost for such projects again fell heavily on state revenues and, indirectly, on the serfs.

Foreign musicians, architects, and artists were welcomed at Elizabeth's court. This influx of European culture continued the Westernization trend initiated by Peter the Great. Russian nobles, hoping to gain favor, often followed Elizabeth's lead. They imitated French manners, learned new languages, and built luxurious houses. However, these cultural developments did little to change the everyday hardships of peasants in the countryside. The empire's wealth was concentrated among the nobility, while the majority population experienced unending labor and escalating demands.

Military Engagements

Elizabeth's reign was not without warfare. Russia became involved in the War of the Austrian Succession (1740–1748) and later the Seven Years' War (1756–1763). These conflicts pitted European powers against each other, reshaping alliances and borders. Elizabeth, a staunch opponent of Prussia's Frederick the Great, poured resources into supporting Austria and France. While Russian troops won notable victories, the wars drained the treasury, led to high casualties, and demanded heavy taxes. Many young serfs were conscripted into the army, leaving their families and lands behind, often forever.

These wars also revealed the efficiency of the empire's administrative system in mobilizing men and supplies. Although Russia at times performed poorly on the battlefield, it still managed to field large armies. The high cost of sustaining these conflicts meant that peasants and townspeople felt additional burdens. When Elizabeth died in 1762, the financial strain and social tensions were poised to burst into new forms of unrest.

Rise of Catherine the Great

The Coup Against Peter III

Elizabeth died childless, and the throne passed to her nephew, Peter III, who was the grandson of Peter the Great's daughter, Anna Petrovna, and a German duke.

Peter III was more German than Russian in his upbringing. He admired Prussia's Frederick the Great, whom Elizabeth had been fighting in the Seven Years' War. Almost immediately upon taking the throne, Peter III ended Russia's conflict with Prussia, a move that shocked the military and many nobles. He also introduced reforms that alienated the church and sections of the nobility.

Peter III's wife, Catherine, was a German princess named Sophia of Anhalt-Zerbst before her conversion to Orthodoxy. Ambitious and politically astute, she saw how unpopular her husband's policies were. In June 1762, factions of the Imperial Guard and high-ranking nobles staged a coup to dethrone Peter III, proclaiming Catherine as Empress. Peter III was forced to abdicate and died soon after under mysterious circumstances. Many believed he was murdered on orders from Catherine's supporters. Catherine took the throne as Catherine II, later celebrated as Catherine the Great.

Early Moves and Consolidation

Upon becoming empress, Catherine presented herself as a champion of Russian interests. She restored privileges to nobles that her husband had curtailed, gaining their loyalty. She also skillfully won the support of the military and the Orthodox Church, distributing promotions and gifts. While she had come to power through a violent coup, Catherine worked to legitimize her reign by emphasizing her commitment to Russia's welfare and stability.

In her early years, Catherine continued some Westernizing policies. She read works by Enlightenment thinkers like Voltaire and Diderot, even corresponding with them. Her court reflected a blend of European intellectual currents and traditional Russian grandeur. For a time, many believed that Catherine might enact major reforms, possibly even alleviating the burdens on peasants or addressing corruption in the administration. However, the reality turned out more complex.

Catherine the Great's Reforms and Ambitions

The Legislative Commission and the "Nakaz"

Early in her reign, Catherine convened the Legislative Commission in 1767, inviting representatives from various social estates—nobles, clergy, merchants, and some peasant communities—to discuss possible reforms. Catherine's "Nakaz" (Instruction) was a guiding document for this commission, influenced by Enlightenment ideas. It spoke of reason, the importance of law, and the well-being of the people. For a moment, it seemed Russia might move toward a more rational and humane legal system.

Yet, the commission ran into obstacles. Nobles refused to diminish their own privileges. The peasants' voices, though theoretically invited, had little real power. Catherine realized that challenging the nobility could lead to political backlash. She dissolved the Legislative Commission without implementing significant changes, signaling that while she admired Enlightenment philosophy, she would not risk her throne to bring about real social transformation.

Expansionist Goals

Catherine turned her attention to expanding Russia's borders. Under her rule, Russia fought successful wars against the Ottoman Empire, gaining access to the

Black Sea coast. This allowed the empire to found new ports, such as Odessa, which boosted trade. Catherine also participated in the partitions of Poland (1772, 1793, and 1795) alongside Prussia and Austria, effectively erasing Poland as a sovereign state for over a century. Russia gained substantial territories and populations through these partitions, and Catherine secured a buffer zone to protect Russia's western frontier.

These territorial gains increased Russia's international standing. They also brought new peoples under Russian rule, including many who were Catholic, Muslim, or Jewish. While Catherine presented herself as a tolerant ruler, many of these communities faced pressures to conform to Russian administrative systems. Local elites were co-opted or replaced, and peasants in newly annexed lands often found themselves under the same heavy-handed control that defined life in the Russian heartland.

Court Intrigue and the Reality of Serfdom

Lavish Court Life

Catherine's court became known for its luxury and brilliance. She entertained European philosophers and corresponded with them, sending gifts and invitations in hopes of displaying Russia's cultural advancement. Masquerade balls, theatrical performances, and opulent banquets were regular events. Nobles competed to impress the empress with expensive clothes and refined manners, while foreign diplomats wrote admiringly of her intelligence and charm.

Beneath this glitter, however, lurked continuous court rivalries. Courtiers sought favor through flattery and by spying on one another. Catherine herself relied on a small circle of trusted advisors and favorites, such as Grigory Orlov and later Grigory Potemkin. Rumors of romantic liaisons circulated, yet Catherine maintained firm control. She rewarded loyalty with grants of land and serfs, further bolstering the nobility's power.

The Worsening Plight of Serfs

For the majority of Russians who worked the land, Catherine's reign did not bring relief. In fact, serfdom grew more entrenched. Catherine handed out vast estates to nobles, often including the peasants living on them. Landlords obtained near-total authority over their serfs, who could be bought, sold, or punished at will. The demand for agricultural produce to support the military and the newly acquired territories pushed landowners to extract more labor. Legal avenues for peasants to complain were practically nonexistent.

Some estates experimented with new farming methods or introduced partial reforms to boost productivity, but these did not change the underlying system. If serfs resisted or tried to flee, punishments ranged from public beatings to exile in Siberia. In times of war or crisis, landlords simply tightened their grip. While Catherine spoke eloquently about justice and the rule of law, her policies ensured the nobility's continued dominance over millions of peasants.

Repression of Dissent

Secret Police and Surveillance

Catherine the Great, like many autocrats, relied on an extensive network of informants and secret police to root out opposition. Writers or intellectuals who criticized the monarchy risked arrest and exile. Some ended up in remote monasteries, effectively silenced. The empress saw the free exchange of ideas as beneficial only up to the point where it did not threaten her power.

Newspapers and journals needed official approval, and any sign of sedition was swiftly punished. Even foreign works deemed too radical were censored. While Catherine portrayed herself as an enlightened ruler, she recognized that certain Enlightenment ideas—like popular sovereignty—could undermine her authority. As a result, the intellectual freedoms she championed in theory were carefully curbed in practice.

Handling of Rebellious Provinces

Throughout Catherine's reign, there were local revolts by serfs and minority groups protesting harsh conditions. Each time, the government cracked down with severity. Troops were dispatched to restore order, and rebel leaders faced brutal punishments. An undercurrent of tension simmered in the countryside, fueled by rumors of a ruler who might end serfdom or by false messiahs promising relief. These tensions would explode in a massive uprising known as Pugachev's Rebellion (1773–1775), covered in the next chapter. This rebellion would challenge Catherine's rule and showcase the anger building in rural Russia.

Foreign Affairs and Enlightened Image

Patronage of the Arts and Learning

To solidify her legacy as an enlightened monarch, Catherine sponsored arts, education, and charity projects. She founded the Smolny Institute for Noble Maidens, which provided education for young women of the aristocracy. She expanded the Imperial Library and collected European art, aiming to make St. Petersburg a center of culture. Composers, painters, and architects thrived under her patronage, leaving a lasting cultural imprint on the empire.

Catherine also invited European intellectuals, including the French philosopher Denis Diderot, to her court. These visits fueled the notion that Russia was on par with leading European powers culturally. Diderot, for instance, admired Catherine's intelligence and flattery, yet he remained critical of serfdom. Despite his arguments, the empress showed little inclination to overhaul the system that kept her nobles loyal.

Wars with the Ottoman Empire

Another major focus was the ongoing conflict with the Ottoman Empire. Catherine's ambition to secure warm-water ports on the Black Sea led to significant territorial acquisitions in regions like the Crimea and the Kuban. The wars against the Ottomans were costly, but Russia's successes elevated Catherine's reputation as a powerful ruler. She commissioned grand monuments and celebrations to commemorate victories, reinforcing the image of a triumphant empire.

These expansions also brought Muslim populations under Russian rule. While Catherine initially proclaimed religious tolerance, local elites in newly conquered areas often faced heavy-handed governance. The empire built fortresses, stationed troops, and sometimes forced local leaders to cooperate in a system that resembled a military occupation. Occasionally, this led to revolts, which were met with the same repressive tactics used elsewhere.

Conclusion

Empress Elizabeth and Catherine the Great both presided over courts of extraordinary luxury and spectacle. Elizabeth's ascent to the throne via a coup d'état showed how unstable the Russian succession could be, and her reign highlighted the power of personal loyalty among the guards regiments. Under her watch, Russia continued the process of Westernization, though it remained deeply rooted in the structures of autocracy and serfdom. Her wars burdened the populace, but her lavish lifestyle endeared her to the nobility, who benefited from her patronage.

Catherine the Great, seizing power in her own coup, took the empire to new heights in terms of territory and cultural sophistication. She saw herself as an enlightened monarch, conversing with leading European thinkers. Yet the same Catherine strengthened the nobility's grip on serfs and suppressed opposition with secret police and censorship. She expanded Russia's borders through wars and partitions, showcasing her ability to wield power on the international stage. Her achievements, however, rested on a foundation of forced labor and the unbroken will of an autocratic state apparatus.

CHAPTER 8

PUGACHEV'S REBELLION AND THE WIDENING GULF BETWEEN CLASSES

Introduction

During the reign of Catherine the Great, Russia underwent significant expansion and embraced Enlightenment ideals—at least on the surface. Yet this period also saw increasing demands on serfs and a growing sense of frustration among peasants, Cossacks, and oppressed minorities. The state, led by Catherine, allied ever more closely with the nobility, granting them further control over those who worked the land. Taxes were high, military conscription was relentless, and a rigid social hierarchy left millions with little hope for improvement.

It was in this environment that a Cossack named Emelyan Pugachev emerged, claiming to be the murdered Tsar Peter III. He promised to free the serfs and distribute land to the common people. His message echoed across the Volga River region, the Ural Mountains, and beyond. What began as a small Cossack uprising in 1773 quickly swelled into a major revolt. Vast stretches of territory fell under rebel control, and local officials were driven out or killed. For a brief moment, it seemed Pugachev might challenge the very foundation of Catherine's rule.

However, the Imperial Army eventually rallied, crushing the rebellion in a series of battles. The government's response was brutal—thousands were executed or punished, villages were burned, and the fear of peasant uprisings intensified. Pugachev's Rebellion served as a stark warning about the explosive anger simmering among the lower classes. It also led Catherine to strengthen her ties with the nobility even further, ensuring that the institution of serfdom would become more entrenched. In this chapter, we will trace the origins, key events, and ultimate defeat of Pugachev's Rebellion. We will also explore the horrifying acts committed by both rebels and government forces, revealing the depths of desperation and cruelty in 18th-century Russia.

Background: Growing Tensions Under Catherine

The Burden on Serfs

By the mid-18th century, serfdom in Russia had evolved into a crushing system of oppression. Landlords possessed near-total authority over their serfs, who could be bought, sold, or punished without recourse. Military conscription also took a heavy toll. Entire villages lost young men to lifetime service in the Imperial Army. War demands meant increased taxation, with little left for the peasant families themselves. Stories of brutal landlords circulated widely, including accounts of torture, forced marriages, and sexual exploitation. Some peasants tried to flee to frontier areas such as the Don region or Siberia, but the state kept extending its reach, making escape ever more difficult.

Cossack Discontent

Cossacks traditionally inhabited frontier regions, enjoying a degree of autonomy in exchange for providing military service when called upon. However, Catherine's government gradually encroached on their freedoms, introducing stricter administrative controls and trying to integrate Cossack lands into the empire's bureaucratic system. The Yaik Cossacks (later known as the Ural Cossacks) near the Ural River were among those feeling the squeeze. Disputes with local officials over fishing rights, trade, and taxes festered, sparking resentment against St. Petersburg's authority.

A few small uprisings flared before 1773, but these were quickly suppressed. The local population bore grudges against officials who extorted bribes or forcibly conscripted men into the army. The seeds of larger rebellion were planted in this climate of anger and frustration. All it needed was a spark—and a leader who could rally various discontented groups under a single cause.

Emelyan Pugachev: The False Peter III

A Charismatic Leader

Emelyan Pugachev was a Don Cossack with some military experience. He had served in the Russo-Turkish War but deserted due to the hardships and brutal discipline. Restless and embittered, Pugachev traveled across the steppe region, meeting peasants, Cossacks, and Old Believers—groups often at odds with the central government. In 1773, he appeared among the Yaik Cossacks, proclaiming himself to be Tsar Peter III, the husband of Catherine the Great who had been deposed and supposedly killed. Claiming that he had escaped assassination, Pugachev promised to restore true justice to Russia.

This bold claim resonated with people who despised the current regime. Rumors had long circulated that Peter III might still be alive, and the legend of a "hidden tsar" had deep roots in Russian folklore. Pugachev declared that he would end the tyranny of landlords and free the peasants from serfdom. He also pledged to reduce taxes, halt forced conscription, and deliver vengeance upon corrupt nobles and officials. In a society where the vast majority had no avenue for expressing discontent, these promises ignited hope.

The Spark That Lit the Steppe

The Yaik Cossacks rallied to Pugachev's cause first, attacking local outposts and driving out imperial officials. Pugachev's forces seized weapons, ammunition, and supplies. Peasants soon joined, drawn by the chance to overthrow the lords who exploited them. Some were driven by desperation, others by genuine belief that Pugachev was the rightful tsar who would reward their loyalty. Many Old Believer communities, persecuted by the state church, also saw Pugachev as a liberator.

As the rebellion grew, Pugachev set up a makeshift court, appointing "ministers" and issuing decrees in the name of Tsar Peter III. He promised land to peasants and freedom from landlords. Peasant rebels attacked noble estates, burning manor houses and sometimes killing landowners and their families. Stories of atrocities circulated quickly, stoking fear among the nobility. At the same time, the rebels cheered Pugachev's proclamations, convinced they were on the verge of a new era.

Early Successes of the Rebellion

Seizing Fortresses and Towns

From the autumn of 1773 through 1774, Pugachev's forces captured multiple fortresses along the Yaik River and in the Ural region. Garrisons either surrendered due to being outnumbered or switched sides. The rebels marched into towns, freeing prisoners and announcing the end of taxes and serfdom. Bureaucrats and noble landlords fled in panic, unless they were caught and summarily executed by vengeful crowds.

The Cossack rebels demonstrated effective mobility, using their knowledge of local terrain to outmaneuver imperial troops. Peasants in the countryside provided food and shelter, grateful for a chance to strike back at the ruling class. In the eyes of many, Pugachev had fulfilled the legendary role of a "good tsar," defending the oppressed against cruel nobles and corrupt officials.

Brutal Attacks on Nobles and Officials

While many peasants saw the rebellion as a chance for justice, the chaos led to horrifying acts of violence. Rebels would sometimes drag captured noble families into public squares, subjecting them to humiliations and executions. Manor houses were looted or burned, their treasures scattered. Local government offices were ransacked, and documents that symbolized oppressive taxes or obligations were destroyed.

Pugachev's aim to unify different factions under his banner led him to sanction severe reprisals against anyone who resisted. These actions served as both vengeance and a warning, fueling the rebellion's momentum. However, they also hardened the resolve of the state to crush the movement. Terrifying accounts of peasant violence spread among the upper classes, convincing them that no compromise was possible.

Catherine's Response

Mobilizing the Imperial Army

News of Pugachev's victories alarmed Catherine the Great and her advisors. Initially, the government underestimated the scale of the uprising, sending smaller detachments of troops that were easily overwhelmed. But as fortress after fortress fell to the rebels, Catherine recognized the threat. She mobilized larger forces, including regular army regiments and artillery, and dispatched them under experienced generals. The empire's organizational capacity allowed the government to raise new units quickly, pulling in reinforcements from more stable regions.

These troops were often better trained and equipped than the rebel forces. Nonetheless, they had to contend with vast distances, poor roads, and unfamiliar terrain. Many officers came from noble families who felt personally endangered by the rebellion. That sense of urgency drove them to show no mercy when retaking rebel-held towns.

Propaganda and Offers of Amnesty

Catherine also used propaganda to undermine Pugachev's credibility. Decrees circulated proclaiming him an impostor and condemning his followers as criminals. Tales of rebel atrocities were exaggerated to frighten potential supporters. At the same time, Catherine offered amnesty to peasants who surrendered, promising lenient treatment if they abandoned Pugachev. The real purpose was to sow doubt among the rebels and isolate their leaders.

These tactics had mixed results. Some peasants, fearful of the imperial army's approach, laid down their arms. Others remained loyal to Pugachev, seeing no future under the old system of serfdom. Many believed Catherine's amnesty was a trick, since they had already participated in attacks on officials and nobles. With the lines drawn, both sides prepared for a brutal confrontation.

Climax and Collapse of the Rebellion

March on Kazan

One of Pugachev's boldest moves was his march on Kazan, a major trading and administrative center on the Volga River. The city was well-fortified and housed a significant population, including many wealthy merchants and nobles. If Pugachev could capture Kazan, he would gain both immense resources and a powerful symbolic victory. For a short time, rebels did break into parts of the city, burning buildings and causing chaos. However, imperial forces regrouped and launched a counterattack. Street-by-street fighting pushed the rebels back, and Pugachev's army retreated. Kazan lay in partial ruins, but it did not fall completely into rebel hands.

This setback proved damaging to Pugachev's aura of invincibility. Imperial authorities quickly reinforced the region, cutting off rebel supply lines. Peasants who had been on the fence now hesitated, seeing that the government might triumph after all.

Defeat on the Steppe

Retreating from Kazan, Pugachev attempted to cross the Volga and rally more peasants, aiming possibly to reach the Don region for fresh support. But Catherine's generals pursued relentlessly. The rebels' numbers were still large, but they faced shortages of ammunition and disunity. Different factions within the rebellion argued over tactics and loot. Imperial troops closed in, benefiting from better coordination and supplies.

In a crucial battle near Tsaritsyn (modern-day Volgograd), Pugachev's forces suffered a decisive defeat. Survivors scattered into the steppes. Betrayed by some of his own followers who hoped to save themselves, Pugachev was captured in late 1774. Dragged to Moscow in chains, he was displayed as a prize—proof that the "impostor tsar" had been subdued.

Horrors of the Aftermath

Punishments and Executions

Catherine's government exacted vicious reprisals. Pugachev himself was executed publicly in January 1775 in Moscow. He was tortured, drawn, and quartered—an old and gruesome form of capital punishment meant to send a chilling message. Other rebel leaders met similar fates. Thousands of peasants, Cossacks, and villagers deemed complicit faced execution, exile, or forced labor. Entire settlements were razed, with families torn apart and survivors deported to distant parts of the empire.

The brutality extended beyond rebel leaders. Imperial troops carried out mass killings in areas suspected of supporting the uprising. Women and children were not always spared. Some accounts describe soldiers setting fire to houses with inhabitants still inside, or forcing captured rebels to watch as their families were punished. Fear reigned, and many who had joined the rebellion or sympathized with it realized there would be no mercy.

Stricter Controls

In the rebellion's wake, Catherine implemented a series of administrative changes, aiming to prevent future uprisings. The government reorganized provincial governance, placing more power in the hands of appointed governors and noble councils. The autonomy of Cossack communities was severely curtailed. New regulations tightened the state's grip on local affairs, so that any hint of unrest could be crushed early.

Serfdom remained firmly in place—if anything, it became more entrenched. The lesson learned by the nobility was that giving peasants any taste of freedom or rights could invite chaos. Landlords felt justified in enforcing discipline more harshly, to keep potential rebellion at bay. Catherine, despite her Enlightenment facade, saw the necessity of relying on noble power to maintain order, reinforcing the existing social hierarchy.

Consequences and Legacy

A Warning to the Empire

Pugachev's Rebellion was the largest and bloodiest peasant uprising in Russia before the 20th century. It demonstrated the deep hatred many serfs and Cossacks felt toward the exploitative system. Though it failed, the scale of the revolt showed the empire's vulnerability. If a single charismatic leader could rally peasants, Cossacks, and other discontented groups, the throne could be seriously threatened.

For Catherine, the rebellion proved that noble support was crucial to her rule. She enacted further policies that favored the nobility, granting them more privileges in exchange for loyalty. This approach locked the empire into a structure where serfdom was vital to economic and social stability—at least from the perspective of the ruling elite.

Impact on Future Reforms

Catherine's subsequent actions to reform governance were mostly administrative. She divided Russia into new provinces and districts, each with improved bureaucracy and more effective policing. However, she avoided any challenge to serfdom. The events of the rebellion convinced her and the nobility that letting peasants gain more freedoms was too dangerous. Future tsars, including Alexander I and Nicholas I, would grapple with the memory of this uprising when considering whether to reform or abolish serfdom. The fear of another massive revolt hung over the empire's leadership.

In literature and folk songs, Pugachev became a legendary figure—both demonized as a savage rebel and romanticized as a champion of the downtrodden. Among peasants, stories circulated that he had been a "true tsar" who tried to end their suffering. This folklore kept alive the hope that one day, someone else might arise to free them from bondage.

CHAPTER 9

PAUL I'S TURBULENT REIGN AND RUTHLESS POLICIES

Introduction

Catherine the Great's long reign ended in 1796, leaving behind an expansive empire that had grown in territory and prestige. Although she maintained a glittering court and embraced elements of Enlightenment thought, she also upheld—indeed strengthened—serfdom and preserved the privileges of the nobility. When Catherine died, the Russian throne passed to her son, Paul I. Paul had lived much of his life in the shadow of his formidable mother. From his youth, he was kept away from key government affairs, fueling resentment and a deep-seated sense of isolation.

Upon taking the crown, Paul I quickly showed the empire that he would not simply continue Catherine's policies. He regarded many of his mother's reforms with suspicion and sought to reassert the authority of the crown in ways that shocked the nobility. Over the course of his short reign (1796–1801), Paul introduced sweeping changes—some aimed at the aristocracy, others at the army, and all with the ultimate goal of establishing a more tightly controlled state under his direct command. However, his eccentric behavior, sudden decrees, and harsh punishments earned him many enemies. Nobles, military officers, and even members of his own court eventually conspired against him, leading to a dramatic end that highlighted how precarious autocratic power could be when wielded impulsively.

In this chapter, we will explore the background of Paul I's life under Catherine, the nature of his ascension to the throne, and the policies he tried to enforce. We will examine how his attempts to centralize authority alienated powerful aristocrats, and how his unpredictable rule created a climate of fear throughout the empire. We will delve into examples of his ruthless policies, focusing on the punishments he meted out and the discontent they stirred among both high and low ranks. Finally, we will recount the coup that ended his reign, shedding light on the motivations of those who plotted against him and on the violent manner in which his rule was terminated. Through this story, we see how power, fear, and personal vengeance converged to create one of the most tumultuous chapters in the history of imperial Russia.

Paul's Early Years and Relationship with Catherine

A Complicated Childhood

Paul was born in 1754, the only son of the future Catherine the Great (then Grand Duchess Ekaterina Alexeevna) and her husband, the Grand Duke Peter (later Peter III). From the start, questions surrounded his parentage—rumors circulated that he might not be Peter's son at all, but rather the product of one of Catherine's liaisons. This speculation, though never proven, would dog him in later years and feed into his deep insecurity.

Catherine's relationship with her son was distant at best. After she seized power in 1762 by overthrowing her husband, Peter III, she kept Paul away from direct involvement in governance. She feared that if he gained too much popularity or influence, factions at court might use him as a figurehead against her. Paul's education was carefully supervised, but he often felt starved for genuine parental affection. The Empress entrusted him to tutors who emphasized strict discipline, shaping a prince who oscillated between obedience, frustration, and a craving for recognition.

Frustration in the Shadows

As Paul grew into adolescence and then adulthood, he watched Catherine's court from the outside. Despite his status as heir, his mother rarely entrusted him with significant responsibilities. He was married off—first to Natalia Alexeievna (who died in childbirth), then to Maria Feodorovna—but these arrangements did little to give him any real power. Instead, he lived on one of his estates, frequently changing the routines of his household according to his personal whims.

During these years, Paul developed a fascination with chivalric ideals and military discipline. He admired the Knightly Orders of Europe and saw the army as a model for obedience and hierarchy. He also nurtured a sense of moral and social justice that was partly shaped by Enlightenment texts, yet heavily filtered through his own distrust of the aristocracy. By the time Catherine died, Paul had compiled a long list of grievances against the nobility she favored, and he firmly believed that Russia needed a more rigid and disciplined approach to governance.

Ascension to the Throne

Catherine's Death and Paul's Surprise

Catherine the Great passed away unexpectedly on November 17, 1796 (November 6, Old Style). She had reportedly been drafting plans to bypass Paul in the line of succession, perhaps favoring her grandson, Alexander, whom she had personally educated. But she died before finalizing these arrangements. As a result, Paul legally ascended to the throne without immediate challenge.

From the moment Paul learned of his mother's death, he seemed determined to set himself apart from her. The funeral arrangements for Catherine were opulent, but Paul also ordered the exhumation of his father, Peter III, so that Peter's remains could lie in state beside Catherine's—a macabre gesture that symbolically reunited the couple. This act was widely interpreted as Paul's attempt to legitimize both his own claim and Peter III's memory, effectively undermining Catherine's portrayal of Peter as weak and unfit.

Early Moves and Symbolic Gestures

Paul wasted no time in broadcasting his new vision for the empire. He reversed several of Catherine's policies—some petty, some more substantial—seemingly to prove his independence. For instance, he repealed Catherine's Charter to the Nobility, a document that had granted significant liberties and privileges to aristocrats. He also ordered changes in court dress, ceremonial protocols, and even the design of uniforms, reflecting his obsession with precise military order.

The new emperor surrounded himself with a coterie of trusted advisors who shared his emphasis on discipline and loyalty. He sought to root out corruption in state administration, and for a short while, some officials saw him as a reform-minded ruler determined to correct Catherine's excesses. Yet Paul's mercurial nature quickly led him to issue conflicting orders, instill fear among those who served him, and punish perceived opposition with startling severity.

Paul I's Policies and the Drive for Control

Centralization of Authority

One of Paul's core beliefs was that Russia suffered from too much aristocratic independence. During Catherine's reign, nobles had enjoyed broad freedoms, including the right not to serve in the army or bureaucracy if they so chose. Paul considered this a danger to the autocracy. He resolved to tighten the reins by:

1. **Reinstating Mandatory Service**: Noble families were once again expected to provide military officers or state officials. Refusal to comply risked severe penalties.
2. **Eliminating Favoritism**: Paul distrusted the high-born elites of Catherine's court, many of whom had become wealthy through imperial patronage. He dismissed or sidelined individuals who had thrived under his mother's rule, replacing them with officials he believed were more loyal or more straightforward.
3. **Enforcing Rigid Hierarchy**: The court was subject to detailed regulations on dress, etiquette, and procedures. Even minor infractions could lead to punishment or demotion. This militaristic approach extended beyond the palace, with government institutions pressed to adopt stricter methods of oversight.

Military Reforms

Paul's obsession with military discipline became a hallmark of his reign. He introduced the Prussian-style military drill and uniform, instructing soldiers on meticulous marching steps, posture, and grooming. Regiments that had served Catherine loyally were reshuffled, with new officers promoted. This caused deep resentment among veterans who felt their experience and tradition were being cast aside in favor of Paul's personal preferences.

Moreover, the emperor had little tolerance for any sign of dissent or sloppiness within the armed forces. Punishments included flogging, demotion to the ranks, or even forced labor. The emphasis on form over practical readiness undermined morale. At the same time, Paul's quick changes in military command and strategy generated confusion and unpredictability, leading many to quietly question his judgment.

Restrictions on Western Ideas

Despite his admiration for certain aspects of European military discipline, Paul grew wary of liberal ideas emanating from the West, especially in the wake of the French Revolution. He feared that revolutionary doctrines could spread to Russia's educated elites, spurring unrest or even a challenge to autocracy. Consequently, he tightened censorship on books, newspapers, and imported literature. Certain foreign works, deemed too radical, were banned outright.

Travel abroad was also more regulated. Students and nobles seeking to journey to Europe for education or leisure needed explicit permission, which was not always granted. Informants were employed to monitor gatherings where political discussions might take place. This clampdown on intellectual life frustrated those who had grown used to the relative freedom of Catherine's later years, intensifying a sense that Paul was building a repressive regime.

Tensions with the Nobility

Overturning the Charter to the Nobility

Catherine's Charter to the Nobility had granted wide-ranging privileges, including exemption from corporal punishment and the freedom to leave state service. By nullifying or weakening these privileges, Paul signaled that the nobility's status was contingent on absolute loyalty to the throne. He also empowered local officials to discipline nobles who failed to comply with his directives, a move that eroded the sense of security the aristocracy had enjoyed for decades.

Suddenly, aristocrats who had been living leisurely—relying on serf labor and old family titles—found themselves subject to strict rules and forced to re-enter military or administrative roles. Those who resisted or complained were humiliated in public or exiled to distant provinces. The social fabric of high society, once centered on Catherine's luminous court life, became strained under Paul's watchful eye.

Personal Vendettas and Humiliations

Paul's dissatisfaction was not purely political; it was also personal. Certain families had openly favored Catherine's fatherly stance toward them, while Paul had felt marginalized. Now, as emperor, he used his power to exact revenge. He might, for example, summon a noble to his palace late at night, berate him over a minor infraction, and send him away stripped of rank. In some instances, entire estates were confiscated without due process, with the property owners given little or no recourse.

Such actions spread fear among the upper classes. Gossip soared behind closed doors, as aristocrats worried they might be next. Indeed, many found themselves trying to guess Paul's moods and preferences, hoping to avoid his wrath. This constant unease contributed to growing resentment, and it paved the way for conspiratorial whispers among those who believed that removing Paul was the only solution to restoring stability.

Harsh Punishments and a Climate of Fear

The Scope of Repression

Though Paul's heaviest hand fell on the nobility and military, ordinary citizens also felt the pressure of a paranoid and authoritarian regime. Minor bureaucrats, shopkeepers, and even serfs could be punished if they were suspected of mocking the emperor or disregarding his numerous edicts. Tales spread of travelers arrested for wearing clothing that Paul considered "French," or for using terms associated with revolutionary ideas. In the countryside, officials tightened their grip, ensuring peasants toiled uninterrupted and that taxes reached the treasury.

Deserters from the army or individuals who defied local governors faced brutal sentences. Some were sent to remote garrisons in Siberia; others endured public floggings or mutilations as an example to the populace. Though these methods were not new to autocratic Russia, Paul's unpredictability heightened their chilling effect.

Religious Dimensions

While Paul identified with strict Orthodoxy, he also had curious sympathies for certain chivalric and Catholic influences, especially in relation to the Knights of Malta. He famously declared himself Grand Master of the Order of St. John of Jerusalem (the Knights Hospitaller) in 1798, a bizarre move for a Russian Orthodox ruler. This step confused the clergy and alienated some staunchly Orthodox believers. At the same time, Paul took measures to ensure that the church in Russia remained submissive to state authority, showing no tolerance for dissenting religious figures who questioned him.

Among Old Believer communities, rumors circulated that Paul might grant them more tolerance. Some small gestures were made toward religious minorities, but these were overshadowed by the state's broader policies of control. Ultimately, Paul's stance on religion was as contradictory and erratic as many of his other policies.

Foreign Policy Shifts and Conflicts

Alliances and Abrupt Changes

Paul inherited a complex international situation. Catherine had waged wars against the Ottoman Empire, expanded Russian influence in Europe, and maintained a careful balancing act with major powers such as Austria and Great Britain. Initially, Paul continued some of these alignments, positioning Russia against Revolutionary France. However, his growing distrust of England and other allies led him to shift course drastically.

At one point, he seemed to consider an alliance with Napoleonic France, seeing Britain as a dangerous rival. This reversal caused alarm among Russian generals who had been fighting the French. It also upset British diplomats and merchants, who feared a trade embargo. Paul's erratic foreign policy moves compounded the sense that he was unreliable and impulsive. Some historians argue that Britain tacitly supported efforts to remove him from power because of his unpredictable stances.

The Maltese Affair

Paul's self-declared role as the Grand Master of the Knights Hospitaller was part of his larger plan to forge a chivalric bond with European monarchs. In 1798,

Napoleon had conquered Malta, displacing the Knights. Paul offered them refuge in Russia and then assumed their leadership in an almost theatrical manner. This baffled many in his court, who found the Catholic order incompatible with Russian Orthodoxy. Others saw it as a sign of Paul's desire for a grandiose image on the international stage. Ultimately, the "Maltese affair" reinforced the perception of Paul as a monarch governed by personal whims rather than diplomatic calculation.

The Road to Conspiracy

Noble Discontent Turns to Plotting

By late 1800, the frustration among Russia's leading families had reached a boiling point. High-ranking officials, generals, and aristocrats saw Paul as a threat to the stability of the empire—and to their own positions. Some believed that if left unchecked, Paul would destroy Russia's alliances, humiliate the nobility further, and possibly lead the country into disastrous wars or internal chaos.

Behind closed doors, a conspiracy began to form. Figures such as Count Peter von Pahlen (the military governor of St. Petersburg), Nikita Panin, and other influential courtiers and officers were at its core. They hoped to remove Paul from power and install his eldest son, Alexander, who was widely seen as more moderate and more in line with Catherine's legacy. Notably, Alexander was aware of some level of discontent and conspiracy, though it remains debated how much he knew about the specific plan for his father's overthrow.

Encouragement from Abroad?

Although direct evidence is scarce, many contemporaries suspected that foreign powers had an interest in Paul's downfall, especially Britain. Paul's threats to disrupt trade routes and his pivot toward France worried London. While it is not clear if British agents actively participated in the conspiracy, there is strong indication that they turned a blind eye to events that would lead to Paul's removal. Russian aristocrats themselves did not need much external encouragement, as they felt driven by self-preservation and a genuine belief that the emperor's policies endangered the empire.

Paul I's Assassination and Its Aftermath

The Fateful Night

On the night of March 23–24, 1801, the conspirators made their move. A group of officers entered the Mikhailovsky Castle (also known as St. Michael's Castle), Paul's newly built residence in St. Petersburg. They found the emperor in his private chambers. Accounts vary on the precise sequence of events, but it is generally agreed that Paul resisted when they confronted him with demands to sign his abdication. In the ensuing struggle, he was struck and strangled. Some reports even say he was bludgeoned with a snuffbox—an ignominious end for an emperor.

Alexander, Paul's son, was in a nearby room. The conspirators quickly informed him that he was now tsar. Allegedly, Alexander was horrified by his father's murder, but the coup's leaders insisted that the empire needed him. By morning, word spread that Paul I had died of "apoplexy," a claim few believed. The empire braced itself for what would come under the new ruler.

Reactions and the New Tsar's Delicate Position

Publicly, Alexander I mourned his father. He organized a respectable funeral and outwardly condemned the crime. However, behind the scenes, many recognized that he owed his throne to the conspirators. This placed Alexander in a fragile situation. He had to balance the desires of those who had orchestrated the coup with his own need to legitimize himself in the eyes of the broader population. Over time, Alexander distanced himself from the murder's more brutal participants, sending some into retirement or distant postings.

Meanwhile, the nobility breathed a collective sigh of relief. They hoped that the new emperor would restore the privileges Paul had threatened. Indeed, one of Alexander's first actions was to moderate many of Paul's decrees, revive the Charter to the Nobility, and ease censorship. The abrupt shift from a climate of fear to a more conciliatory approach underscored just how swiftly a single assassination could redirect the course of Russian policy.

Legacy of Paul I's Short Reign

Though Paul's reign lasted barely four and a half years, it left a significant mark on Russia. His attempt to impose absolute authority—both on the army and the aristocracy—demonstrated the limitations of autocracy when exercised with unpredictable force and personal vendettas. Paradoxically, some of Paul's ideas foreshadowed future reforms: he disliked the aristocracy's unrestrained power over serfs, and in some isolated cases, he issued rules that restrained the worst abuses of serfdom. However, these measures were overshadowed by his oppressive style and rapid policy shifts that alienated nearly everyone of influence.

Paul's violent end served as a grim reminder that tsars could be overthrown if they lost the support of the powerful classes. His fate echoed those of earlier rulers who fell victim to court intrigues, showing that autocratic power, while immense, was never absolute. In the decades following his death, stories of Paul's bizarre demands and sudden punishments became part of court lore—a cautionary tale about the dangers of unbridled authority mixed with personal paranoia.

CHAPTER 10

THE WAR OF 1812 AND THE MISERY IT LEFT BEHIND

Introduction

Following the assassination of Paul I in 1801, his son Alexander I took the throne. Initially regarded as a liberal-minded ruler, Alexander implemented cautious reforms and entertained grand visions of modernizing Russia. Yet his reign would face a challenge of epic proportions: the rapid expansion of Napoleon Bonaparte's French Empire, which threatened to reorder the entire European continent. Tensions between Russia and France steadily escalated, culminating in the fateful year of 1812, when Napoleon launched a massive invasion of Russian territory.

The resulting conflict, often called the Patriotic War of 1812 in Russian historiography, became one of the most defining moments in the nation's history. Though Napoleon's Grand Army reached Moscow and occupied it briefly, the grueling march, harsh weather, and scorched-earth tactics employed by the Russians spelled disaster for the invaders. For the Russian people, however, "victory" came at a terrible price. The war devastated cities and villages, led to horrific loss of life, and unleashed famine and disease. Refugees flooded the countryside, while peasants struggled to survive as armies trampled the land in search of supplies.

In this chapter, we will examine the origins of the Franco-Russian conflict, chart the major events of the 1812 campaign, and explore the desperate measures both sides undertook. We will look beyond the battlefield to the misery suffered by ordinary Russians—peasants, townspeople, and soldiers alike. We will also assess the war's aftermath, including the profound impact it had on Russian society and government. While the conflict ended with Napoleon's retreat and a wave of nationalist pride, it sowed seeds of discontent that would grow in the years to come, reminding us that even grand patriotic triumphs can leave behind deep scars and painful memories.

Preludes to Invasion

Alexander I's Early Reign and Shifting Alliances

After coming to power, Alexander I surrounded himself with advisors who encouraged moderate reforms, particularly in education and administration. He showed interest in constitutional ideas, though he never fully implemented them. Abroad, Alexander initially aligned Russia with other European powers against Napoleon's ambitions. However, French victories in Central Europe forced him to reconsider. The defeat of Russian forces at Austerlitz (1805) and Friedland (1807) illustrated the strength of Napoleon's army, compelling Alexander to negotiate.

The Treaty of Tilsit (1807) made Russia an uneasy ally of France. Alexander agreed to join the Continental System, a blockade against British trade. This arrangement frustrated Russian nobles and merchants who relied heavily on British commerce. The relationship between the two emperors—Alexander and Napoleon—was marked by suspicion, rivalry, and personal pride. It did not take long for the fragile alliance to unravel.

Escalating Tensions

Several factors led to a breakdown in Franco-Russian relations:

1. **Continental System Woes**: Russia's economy suffered under the blockade, prompting Alexander to relax enforcement. Napoleon viewed this as a betrayal.
2. **Polish Question**: Napoleon created the Duchy of Warsaw in former Polish territories, stoking Russian fears that he might restore a full Polish state on Russia's western border.
3. **Dynastic Ambitions**: Napoleon married Marie Louise of Austria in 1810, distancing himself further from a proposed marriage alliance with Russia.
4. **Mutual Distrust**: Both emperors harbored ambitions for influence in Eastern Europe. Their personal egos and strategic goals clashed, making compromise difficult.

By 1811, diplomatic relations had deteriorated to the point that war seemed inevitable. Napoleon assembled the largest army Europe had yet seen, pulling troops from all over his empire. Russian generals braced for invasion, though disagreements over strategy and command positions weakened their preparedness.

Napoleon's Invasion Begins

The Grande Armée Crosses the Niemen

On June 24, 1812, Napoleon's Grande Armée—estimated at 400,000 to 600,000 soldiers (depending on the source)—crossed the Niemen River, marking the official start of the invasion. The emperor expected a swift campaign. He believed that once the Russian forces were defeated in a few set-piece battles, Alexander would sue for peace. However, the Russian command, led primarily by generals Barclay de Tolly and Bagration, opted for a strategy of gradual retreat rather than risking annihilation in a single engagement.

As the French advanced deeper into Russian territory, they found empty fields and abandoned villages. The Russians employed scorched-earth tactics, destroying crops, livestock, and supplies to deny the invaders sustenance. Civilians often fled in terror, leaving their homes to be burned. This policy, though brutal, was effective in slowing the Grande Armée's progress and eroding its morale.

Smolensk and the Battle of Valutino

Smolensk became one of the first major objectives for Napoleon. The city was an important fortress and a symbolic gateway to Moscow. French forces reached Smolensk in August 1812, engaging in fierce fighting with Russian defenders. Ultimately, the Russians evacuated, setting the city ablaze. Thousands died on both sides, and the burning of Smolensk left a haunting image of devastation. Napoleon pressed on, believing the decisive battle he sought would come soon.

But at Valutino (also called the Battle of Lubino), the retreating Russian army inflicted significant losses on the French. While not a knockout victory, it delayed Napoleon's progress further. Soldiers on both sides endured exhaustion, hunger, and intense summer heat. Already, the Grande Armée found itself stretched thinner than anticipated, its supply lines overextended and harassed by Russian light cavalry.

The Battle of Borodino: A Bloodbath

Gathering Forces Outside Moscow

By early September, Russian forces had combined under the command of General Mikhail Kutuzov. Pressured by public outcry to defend Moscow, Kutuzov decided to make a stand near the village of Borodino, about 125 kilometers west of the capital. The Russians dug in, establishing fortifications such as the Raevsky Redoubt and the Bagration Fleches. Napoleon arrived with his main army, confident that a crushing victory would force Alexander to capitulate.

The stage was set for one of the most lethal one-day battles in history. On September 7, 1812, the Grande Armée launched massive assaults against the Russian positions, and the Russians fought back with desperate tenacity. Artillery barrages pounded both sides, while cavalry charges and bayonet fights added to the carnage. By nightfall, tens of thousands lay dead or wounded. Estimates vary widely, but most agree that each side suffered at least 30,000 casualties.

Outcome and Aftermath

Borodino was, in many ways, a Pyrrhic victory for the French. The Russians eventually withdrew, conceding the field to Napoleon. However, the Russians remained cohesive as a fighting force, and their retreat was orderly. More importantly, the battle inflicted massive losses on the Grande Armée—losses it could not easily replace in hostile territory.

The retreating Russians continued their scorched-earth policy. Civilians in nearby villages had either fled or been conscripted for labor. Fields were burnt, and wells poisoned. The French soldiers who had survived Borodino were exhausted, many suffering from wounds, disease, and faltering morale. Still, Napoleon pushed on toward the fabled capital—Moscow.

The Occupation and Burning of Moscow

Entering the Abandoned City

On September 14, Napoleon entered Moscow expecting a formal surrender. Instead, he found a largely deserted city. Most inhabitants had evacuated, and Governor-General Fyodor Rostopchin had authorized the removal or destruction of valuable supplies. Within days of the French arrival, fires broke out across Moscow, quickly engulfing wooden structures in an inferno. The cause remains disputed—some blame Russian arsonists, while others suspect accidental blazes ignited by retreating soldiers or French looters.

Regardless of who lit the first spark, the result was catastrophic. Much of Moscow burned to the ground, depriving the French of shelter and vital resources. Soldiers scavenged for food and valuables amid smoldering ruins. Napoleon, shocked by the scale of destruction, spent over a month in the ruined capital, hoping Alexander would negotiate peace. But no peace offer came.

Desperate Conditions

As the autumn nights grew colder, French morale plummeted. There was little to eat, and rumors of Russian counterattacks spread. Disorder infected the ranks. Looting and lawlessness became rampant, with some units turning on each other for scarce provisions. Meanwhile, Russian partisans and cavalry units harassed foraging parties on the city's outskirts, capturing stragglers and cutting communication lines. Disease, particularly typhus and dysentery, took root in the cramped quarters where the French soldiers huddled.

Russian peasants in the surrounding countryside were no better off. Many had fled further east, losing their homes and harvests. Others hid in forests or marshlands, living off whatever they could gather. Some formed guerrilla bands to raid isolated French detachments—acts that further infuriated Napoleon's officers, who responded with reprisals against civilians. The entire region descended into chaos and misery, with no clear path to resolution.

The Retreat from Moscow

The Decision to Withdraw

By mid-October, it was apparent to Napoleon that occupying a burned-out Moscow served no purpose. With winter approaching and no sign of a Russian surrender, he reluctantly ordered the retreat. The French began their march out of the city on October 19, carrying wagons overloaded with loot. The plan was to move south toward the fertile regions of Kaluga, hoping to find provisions and reestablish supply lines. Kutuzov, however, anticipated this maneuver. After a sharp clash at Maloyaroslavets, the Russians blocked the southern roads, forcing the French to retreat via the already ravaged Smolensk route.

The Onset of Winter

Winter came early and harsh in 1812. Temperatures plummeted below freezing, and snowstorms lashed the retreating Grande Armée. Thousands of horses died from cold and lack of fodder, forcing soldiers to abandon artillery and wagons. Frostbite became common, with men losing fingers, toes, and entire limbs. Desertions soared. Ragged, hungry, and demoralized, the French columns fell prey to continuous skirmishes by Russian forces.

Horrific scenes unfolded on the roads. Starving men fought each other for scraps of horsemeat. Stragglers froze to death at night, their bodies found in grotesque positions of final agony. Disease ripped through the ranks, while Cossack units circled like wolves, picking off isolated groups. Historians often describe the retreat from Moscow as one of the greatest military disasters ever inflicted upon a major invading force.

Suffering of the Russian People

Displaced Populations and Ruined Lands

While the Russian state celebrated Napoleon's calamity, the war left countless ordinary people destitute. Families who abandoned their homes returned to find them looted or burned. Entire villages in the path of the French army were razed, either by the invaders themselves or by Russian scorched-earth teams. Fields lay barren—crops had been destroyed, and livestock stolen or killed. In the immediate aftermath, famine loomed.

Refugees flooded into towns that had not been directly affected by the fighting, putting strain on local resources. Diseases like cholera and typhus spread among the displaced. Soldiers returning from the front often carried infections back to their home regions. While the monarchy and nobility hailed Russia's survival as a triumph, peasants bore the heaviest cost.

Conscription and Military Losses

Russia's army suffered enormous casualties throughout 1812. While battlefield deaths at Borodino and other engagements were high, disease and exposure claimed even more lives. Many of those conscripted were serfs, forcibly taken from their villages, leaving families struggling to meet labor demands. Although the government and aristocracy lauded these men as patriots, the reality was that most had no choice but to fight.

For those who did survive, the return home could be bittersweet. Some discovered that their families had perished or their lands lay in ruins. Instances of mutiny or desertion spiked in the war's aftermath, as soldiers grew disillusioned with the hardships they faced both during and after their service. This dissatisfaction simmered beneath the surface, planting seeds for future unrest in the Russian Empire.

The Road to Paris and Russia's Post-War Challenges

Pushing Into Europe

Napoleon's defeat did not end with the retreat from Moscow. Alexander I, emboldened by success, joined a coalition of European powers that pursued the

French into Central Europe. A series of battles culminated in the capture of Paris in 1814 and Napoleon's exile to Elba. For Russia, this campaign forged a reputation as the "savior of Europe." Alexander stood at the pinnacle of his influence, shaping post-war Europe at the Congress of Vienna (1814–1815).

Russian forces marched through territories ravaged by years of Napoleonic warfare. While these expeditions earned Russia international prestige, they also stretched the empire's resources. Maintaining armies abroad was expensive, and many soldiers yearned to return home. The famed march to Paris is celebrated in Russian history, but behind the glory lay the burdens placed on ordinary soldiers and taxpayers.

Economic and Social Strain

Despite Russia's newfound status as a great power, the war had wrecked the economy in the immediate term. Agriculture—still the backbone of Russia's wealth—required years of recovery after the scorched-earth tactics. Trade routes had been disrupted, and merchants who depended on exporting goods to Europe found their operations in disarray. Many nobles demanded that serfs work even harder to rebuild estates, intensifying an already oppressive system.

Alexander I, initially praised for leading Russia through the crisis, faced a society grappling with trauma and instability. Veterans returning to their villages often clashed with estate owners, leading to sporadic peasant revolts. Although these were localized and quickly suppressed, they signaled a deeper malaise. People wanted tangible rewards for their sacrifices—less feudal oppression, lower taxes, or better representation. The autocracy offered little of that, focused instead on diplomatic achievements and maintaining the conservative social order.

War's Influence on Russian Identity and Nationalism

The Birth of Patriotic Sentiment

The War of 1812 is often credited with igniting a sense of national consciousness among Russians. Propaganda depicted the conflict as a righteous struggle to defend the motherland and Orthodoxy against a foreign tyrant. The church played a major role in framing Napoleon as an anti-Christian invader. Noble and peasant alike, it was said, had united against a common foe, forging a new spirit of unity.

Yet the concept of "nation" remained heavily shaped by the autocracy and Orthodox Christianity. The tsar was seen as a protector chosen by God. This new patriotism did not necessarily translate into a call for citizen rights or democratic reforms. Instead, it reinforced the idea that Russians should remain loyal to the throne and the church in times of crisis. Ironically, the heavy toll of the war also fueled whispers that the social system needed change. While official propaganda lauded unity, many peasants returned to the harsh reality of serfdom and resented the lack of reward for their sacrifices.

Cultural Reflections

Literature, art, and folk songs began to commemorate 1812 as a heroic epic. Painters depicted scenes of burning Moscow, while poets wrote verses celebrating Russian bravery. Over time, figures like Kutuzov became national heroes, lionized for their role in resisting Napoleon. The war also inspired intellectuals to compare Russia's traditions with Europe's, leading some to champion the uniqueness of Russian culture and governance. This contributed to the rise of Slavophiles, who argued that Russia should reject Western models and preserve its own Orthodox, communal heritage.

On the other hand, the war taught some Russians the strengths of European military and administrative organization. Future reforms, including those under Nicholas I and Alexander II, would take lessons from the 1812 experience, noting the weaknesses in supply, organization, and morale. Still, the immediate aftermath showed that real structural changes—especially regarding serfdom—remained elusive.

The Human Toll and Lingering Trauma

Massive Casualties

Exact figures for the war's casualties differ, but consensus holds that Napoleon lost the bulk of his Grande Armée—only a fraction of the invading force ever left Russia. Russian military losses were also colossal, with estimates ranging from 150,000 to 400,000 killed, plus hundreds of thousands of civilian deaths due to famine, disease, and violence. Many villages never recovered their pre-war population, and orphans or widows became a common sight.

Emotional Scars and Survivor Stories

Narratives of horror and resilience spread among the population. Survivors told of entire families who froze to death or starved. Soldiers recounted how they trudged through snow, wearing rags on their feet, passing the bodies of their comrades. Peasant women remembered looting French supply wagons for food, only to be caught and lashed. The trauma left a deep imprint, shaping local legends and personal identities. While the war eventually turned into a patriotic legend of Russian victory, its immediate aftermath was marked by mourning and hardship on a scale few had ever seen before.

Conclusion

The War of 1812 stands as a pivotal juncture in Russian history, a time when the empire faced near-destruction by Napoleon's seemingly unstoppable force. Against all odds, the Russian armies employed strategic retreats, scorched-earth tactics, and attritional warfare to wear down the Grande Armée. The burning of Moscow, the deadly winter, and relentless harassment by Russian forces ensured that Napoleon's greatest campaign ended in disaster for the French. For the Russian people, however, triumph came wrapped in immense suffering.

Cities like Smolensk and Moscow lay in ruins; countless villages were obliterated. Peasants and townsfolk fled the path of invasion, returning months later to find their homes destroyed. Soldiers who marched with Kutuzov saw friends perish from wounds, disease, or the brutal cold. Many families lost sons to the army or to the ravages of war. Yet, from this catastrophe emerged a stronger sense of Russian identity—one that romanticized the defense of the motherland and reinforced loyalty to the autocracy and the Orthodox faith.

In the years following 1812, Alexander I leveraged Russia's victory to shape the European balance of power, helping lead the coalition that defeated Napoleon for good. But at home, the empire struggled to rebuild amid lingering unrest. The structural inequalities of serfdom and autocratic rule persisted, overshadowing the patriotic fervor. Still, the memory of 1812 took on a life of its own, influencing later generations and becoming a national myth of endurance and unity in the face of mortal danger.

CHAPTER 11

NICHOLAS I AND THE ERA OF STRICT SURVEILLANCE

Introduction

With Napoleon's defeat and the War of 1812 receding into memory, Tsar Alexander I assumed a grand position on the European stage. He became a pivotal figure at the Congress of Vienna and helped shape the new continental order. Yet, in the final years of his reign, Alexander's enthusiasm for reform waned. He grew suspicious of liberal ideas, partly influenced by the turmoil seen in Europe following the French Revolution and the Napoleonic Wars. By the time he died unexpectedly in 1825, Russia had a complex mixture of pride in its military might and deep-seated anxieties about social change.

It was in this climate that Nicholas I, Alexander's younger brother, took the throne. Almost immediately, he faced a startling challenge: the Decembrist Revolt of 1825. Young officers—mainly from noble families—rose up in the name of constitutional governance. Nicholas crushed this uprising with ruthless efficiency. Determined to eliminate subversive tendencies at home and fearful of revolutions abroad, he built a regime known for intense censorship, widespread espionage, and harsh reprisals. Under Nicholas I, Russia's image as a stern autocracy hardened.

This chapter examines the reign of Nicholas I (1825–1855), focusing on the era's pervasive surveillance and control. We will delve into the Decembrist Revolt and its brutal aftermath, the creation of a secret police force that monitored nearly every aspect of public life, and the relentless censorship that stifled intellectual activity. We will also consider how Nicholas's policies affected various segments of society: from nobles who once dreamt of gradual reform, to the peasants who still toiled under serfdom, and the emergent intelligentsia who found themselves under constant watch. As we shall see, Nicholas I's quest for stability led to an environment of fear, leaving a legacy that would cast a long shadow over Russia's future.

The Decembrist Revolt: A Violent Introduction to Nicholas I's Rule

The Confusion of Succession

When Alexander I died in November 1825, the line of succession was not entirely clear. By established law, the crown should have passed to his brother Constantine. However, Constantine had secretly renounced his claim, possibly due to a desire for a quieter life away from the burdens of monarchy. Alexander had then named his younger brother Nicholas as heir. But these decisions were not made public, creating confusion upon Alexander's death. For several weeks, government officials in Saint Petersburg pledged allegiance first to Constantine, then to Nicholas, before the final arrangement became evident.

This confusion gave a group of liberal-minded army officers a window to act. Influenced by Enlightenment ideas and the frustrations that had mounted under Alexander's later conservative turn, they hoped to force constitutional reforms. Many were veterans of the Napoleonic Wars; they had seen Western Europe and believed Russia lagged behind in terms of political rights and civil liberties. They took advantage of the uncertain succession to press for change.

The Revolt on Senate Square

On December 14, 1825 (December 26, New Style), around three thousand soldiers and several officers gathered on Senate Square in Saint Petersburg, refusing to swear allegiance to Nicholas. They demanded a constitution and wanted to install Constantine—whom they presumed would allow such reforms—as the legitimate tsar. Nicholas, alerted to the plot, acted swiftly. He assembled loyal regiments and artillery, surrounding the rebels.

The confrontation turned violent. Nicholas ordered canister shot fired into the crowd, causing chaos and bloodshed. Some rebels fell into the frozen Neva River, drowning after the ice broke beneath them. In a matter of hours, the uprising was crushed. Many of its leaders were arrested on the spot. The event, soon called the Decembrist Revolt (from the month of December), served as a stark signal that Nicholas I would tolerate no challenge to autocracy.

Reprisals and Trials

Nicholas instituted a special commission to investigate the conspiracy. Over a hundred men were put on trial, with varying sentences. Five were hanged—an especially severe sentence in an age when noble-born conspirators were often spared the death penalty. Others were exiled to Siberian labor camps, their families often accompanying them into brutal conditions. Aristocratic families that had once enjoyed prestige found themselves disgraced and stripped of influence.

These punishments shocked much of the nobility. They realized that Nicholas would respond to perceived treason with uncompromising force. The new tsar also saw the revolt as proof that dangerous ideas—constitutionalism, liberalism, republicanism—had taken root among Russia's elite youth. From that moment forward, he resolved to hunt down any hint of subversion. The Decembrists became martyrs in the eyes of later generations of Russian reformers and revolutionaries, but under Nicholas's rule, they were seen as criminals who threatened the very foundations of the empire.

Nicholas I's Ruling Philosophy: "Orthodoxy, Autocracy, Nationality"

The Ideological Triad

The Decembrist Revolt galvanized Nicholas to shape a clear ideology that would guide his reign. In 1833, the minister of education, Sergey Uvarov, formally articulated a doctrine called "Orthodoxy, Autocracy, Nationality" ("Pravoslavie, Samoderzhavie, Narodnost"). It became the official slogan of Nicholas's government, reflecting its emphasis on:

1. **Orthodoxy**: The Russian Orthodox Church was to remain a cornerstone of society, a unifying spiritual and moral force that supported the throne.
2. **Autocracy**: The tsar's power was absolute, divinely ordained, and unchallengeable.
3. **Nationality**: A sense of Russian national identity was championed, extolling the virtues of the peasant masses and traditional culture—while marginalizing or suppressing minority groups if they were seen as a threat.

Consolidating Control

Nicholas's policies enforced this triad in practical ways. The church received extensive support, while religious dissenters (such as Old Believers or sectarians) were pressured to conform. Schools and universities were closely monitored to ensure they instilled loyalty to the autocracy and the Orthodox faith. Textbooks were rewritten to highlight Russia's unique path and to cast suspicion on Western liberal ideas.

Any form of challenge—whether a real conspiracy or simple criticism—was treated as a grave offense. Local governors and police were expected to report suspicious activities or "dangerous thoughts" circulating among students, writers, or salon gatherings. Court ceremonies and official pageantry emphasized the tsar's majesty and paternalistic role over his subjects. These measures aimed to create a fortress of loyalty, where the monarchy, aligned with the church, stood at the apex of Russian civilization.

The Third Section and Secret Police: A Nation Under Watch

Formation of the Third Section

In 1826, Nicholas I established a new branch of his personal chancery known as the Third Section. It served as a secret police force with the mandate to root out any subversive elements. The Third Section had wide-ranging powers: it could spy on private correspondence, infiltrate societies or clubs, and arrest suspects without going through normal legal channels. Informants were cultivated, sowing fear and mistrust among intellectuals, nobles, and bureaucrats.

The agency was led by Count Alexander Benckendorff, a zealous supporter of the tsar, who famously stated: "Where there is no government, there is no fatherland." Under Benckendorff's supervision, the Third Section compiled dossiers on thousands of citizens—nobles who traveled abroad too frequently, students who read forbidden books, professors who questioned official doctrine, and even lesser functionaries who uttered critical remarks at dinner tables. This surveillance network embedded itself in Russian daily life, discouraging open discourse.

The Role of Censorship

Working closely with the Third Section was a rigorous censorship apparatus. Nicholas had little patience for the flourishing literary scene that had blossomed under Alexander I's more lenient approach. Publishers needed government approval, and censors combed through manuscripts before they could be printed. Works by foreign authors perceived as liberal or revolutionary were banned outright or heavily redacted. Even classics by French or German writers could be disallowed if they contained subversive sentiments.

Russian writers, poets, and intellectuals found themselves either self-censoring or taking extreme risks if they dared to critique social conditions. Many turned to subtle allegories or historical themes to voice discontent without openly attacking the regime. Others grew disillusioned, retreating to quiet corners of private life. To publish something critical of official policies was to invite close scrutiny by the Third Section. Penalties ranged from warnings to exile in Siberia or confinement in remote provincial towns.

Impact on Society: Nobles, Peasants, and the Emerging Intelligentsia

Noble Compliance and Discontent

While many nobles initially welcomed Nicholas's crackdown on the Decembrists—fearing revolution—over time, they too chafed under his rigid system. Those who served in the bureaucracy or the military found themselves under constant scrutiny. Promotions hinged on personal loyalty rather than merit. Court etiquette became stifling, with countless rules about who could speak, sit, or address the emperor. A misstep could derail a career.

Some aristocrats tried to flee this suffocating environment by traveling abroad. Yet even that was policed; departing Russia required official permission. Others embraced the superficial aspects of loyalty, wearing medals or adopting the Orthodox persona expected of them, all while hiding private frustrations. A few bolder souls maintained secret reading circles or private salons where liberal ideas might be discussed in hushed tones. If the Third Section got wind of such activities, those involved risked interrogation or exile.

The Peasant Majority Under Tight Control

For the peasantry, life under Nicholas I was a continuation of harsh realities. Serfdom remained deeply entrenched, with little effort by the state to alleviate it. While Nicholas occasionally mused about reform—some historians say he recognized serfdom as a moral and economic blight—he ultimately sided with the conservative landowning nobility who feared peasant uprisings. In practice, peasants continued to labor under burdensome dues, heavy-handed landlords, and minimal legal recourse.

The state's surveillance apparatus reached into the countryside primarily through local officials, who reported any sign of unrest or rumor. Peasant protests were put down swiftly. Some landowners used the government's stance on discipline to justify brutal treatment of serfs, confident that higher authorities would not intervene. The mismatch between the regime's paternalistic rhetoric—Nicholas styled himself the "father" of his people—and the dire conditions most peasants faced contributed to a simmering dissatisfaction, though it rarely erupted into large-scale revolts during Nicholas's time.

The "Intelligentsia" in Embryonic Form

A new social group—the intelligentsia—began to emerge under Nicholas I, although it had to operate in the shadows. These were educated individuals, including writers, scholars, minor officials, and professionals like doctors or lawyers, who shared a sense of responsibility toward societal problems. They were influenced by European philosophy but often lacked formal outlets for political expression due to censorship.

Some became part of a growing trend of "literary clubs" or private circles where poetry, essays, and critiques of serfdom or autocracy were exchanged. Notable literary figures—like Alexander Pushkin, Mikhail Lermontov, Nikolai Gogol—produced works that sometimes slipped subversive ideas past censors through allegory or imaginative settings. Pushkin, for instance, found himself under the watchful eye of the Third Section throughout his adult life. His exile to Mikhailovskoe was a direct result of the regime's discomfort with his perceived liberal leanings. Though the empire cherished its "national poet," it remained anxious about his influence.

State-Building and Expansion: The Price of Order

Bureaucratic Growth

Under Nicholas I, the Russian bureaucracy expanded significantly. He believed in top-down administration, with layers of officials ensuring that his will reached every corner of the empire. Ministries gained specialized departments, each generating mountains of paperwork to track population, tax collection, and potential security threats. A labyrinth of offices and clerks formed, sometimes described as unwieldy, but all justified by the tsar's desire for order.

The system, however, was prone to corruption. Low-paid officials might demand bribes to expedite documents or overlook regulatory violations. Bribery cases occasionally caught Nicholas's attention, and he would punish the offenders harshly—yet the root causes, such as poor salaries and fear-driven compliance, remained. This contradiction—trying to impose absolute moral order while fostering an environment that bred corruption—exemplified many challenges of Nicholas's reign.

Foreign Adventures and Diplomatic Tensions

Nicholas I's foreign policy largely aimed to project Russia as a dominant conservative power in Europe. He styled himself as the "gendarme of Europe," willing to intervene militarily to suppress revolutions that threatened the established order. For instance, he sent Russian troops into Hungary in 1849 to help the Austrian Empire crush a national uprising, demonstrating his commitment to reactionary principles.

Meanwhile, Russia expanded its territory in the Caucasus, battling local peoples such as the Chechens and other mountain tribes in a brutal conflict that would last decades. The conquest of the Caucasus was marked by fierce resistance led by figures like Imam Shamil, and it involved scorched-earth tactics from Russian generals, who devastated local villages to break the spirit of rebellion. This drawn-out struggle drained resources and stoked resentment, illustrating the human cost of Nicholas's imperial ambitions.

The Grip of Censorship Tightens: Cultural and Intellectual Life

Literature Under Watch

Despite heavy censorship, Russian literature experienced a golden age in this period, albeit overshadowed by constant fear. Poets like Pushkin and Lermontov, novelists like Gogol, and playwrights like Aleksandr Griboyedov emerged as giants of Russian letters. Their works often contained veiled critiques of bureaucracy, social injustice, and the hollow pomp of high society.

- **Pushkin's Exile**: Pushkin spent years under partial or full exile, relocated to remote estates or subjected to supervision. Nicholas I himself read and sometimes personally censored Pushkin's works, an arrangement that both highlighted Pushkin's literary importance and symbolized the state's paranoia. Pushkin navigated this relationship with caution, producing coded criticisms in poems such as "The Bronze Horseman," which explores the tension between ordinary individuals and tsarist power (represented by the statue of Peter the Great).

- **Lermontov's Anger**: Mikhail Lermontov, a younger poet and officer, wrote fiery verses lamenting the fate of Russia's genius under oppressive rule. After penning an elegy for Pushkin—who died in a duel that some attributed partly to the atmosphere of court intrigue—Lermontov was sent to the Caucasus front as punishment. There, he encountered the brutal realities of imperial conquest, which fueled darker, more rebellious themes in his writing.

- **Gogol's Satire**: Nikolai Gogol gained acclaim for his satirical portraits of provincial officials, petty bureaucrats, and corrupt practices in works like "Dead Souls" and "The Government Inspector." Though comedic on the surface, these works skewered the incompetence and moral emptiness fostered by Nicholas's rigid bureaucratic system. Censors sometimes missed deeper criticisms beneath Gogol's absurd humor, but the state increasingly monitored him, especially after some officials recognized themselves in his caricatures.

The Philosophical Underground

Censorship pushed philosophically minded Russians to gather privately, discussing German Idealism, French Romanticism, and English liberalism in living rooms and back alleys. These small circles debated whether Russia should adopt Western democratic models or preserve its own "unique path" aligned with Orthodoxy and autocracy. Some groups veered into mystical or religious speculation, while others became hotbeds for more radical ideas.

Notable among the latter were the Petrashevsky Circle in Saint Petersburg, which included the young Fyodor Dostoevsky among its ranks. They read socialist theories, criticized serfdom, and contemplated social reforms. When word reached the Third Section, Nicholas ordered a dramatic crackdown. Members were arrested, subjected to a mock execution ceremony (where they believed they would be shot), and then exiled or imprisoned. This event deeply traumatized Dostoevsky and shaped his future literary works, underscoring the harsh consequences of even mild dissident discussion.

Economic Realities and Seeds of Future Turmoil

Serfdom's Burden

Throughout Nicholas I's reign, agriculture remained the backbone of Russia's economy, with most peasants bound to the land as serfs. These peasants had to provide labor and produce for their landlords or pay heavy dues. Industrial developments in cities like Moscow and Saint Petersburg slowly began, but they were not sufficient to modernize the empire swiftly. Wealthy nobles were hesitant to invest in industrial ventures, preferring to rely on serf labor for their incomes. The result was a stagnant economy that lagged behind other European powers entering the throes of the Industrial Revolution.

Periodic peasant uprisings still occurred, usually in response to brutal treatment by local landowners or new bureaucratic demands. The authorities suppressed these rebellions with ferocity. Nicholas recognized that the system was problematic and considered partial reforms, such as "inventories" that regulated serfs' obligations. But these moves were half-hearted and faced fierce opposition from landowners. Thus, serfdom persisted unchanged, sowing seeds of discontent that would eventually boil over in later decades.

Infrastructure and Military Projects

Nicholas did invest in certain infrastructure projects, notably the construction of the Moscow–Saint Petersburg railway, completed in 1851. While this project signaled a step into the modern age, it also exemplified the top-down approach: built primarily to facilitate state control and military mobilization, rather than to spur widespread economic growth. Road networks and telegraph lines also expanded, but much of Russia remained inaccessible during bad weather, reinforcing the sense that power was concentrated in a few urban centers.

The Russian army under Nicholas I was enormous in size—some estimates place it at over a million men—but it was often ill-equipped and hindered by a rigid command structure that discouraged initiative. Soldiers, many of them serfs conscripted for decades, lived under harsh discipline. While the army served as a formidable police force within the empire's borders, its preparedness for modern warfare would be tested in the coming Crimean War, revealing stark weaknesses.

The Final Years of Nicholas I and the Looming Storm

The 1848 Revolutions in Europe

In 1848, revolutions erupted across Europe, toppling or threatening monarchies in France, Austria, and various German states. Nicholas saw these events as the ultimate vindication of his fears about liberal ideologies. He cracked down even more at home, increasing press restrictions and urging local officials to be vigilant against any ripple effect from European turmoil. Russian troops assisted Austria in crushing the Hungarian Revolution, which further cemented Nicholas's reputation as the staunch defender of conservative order.

The intensification of internal surveillance contributed to a sense of intellectual suffocation among Russia's educated classes. Some fled abroad, while others became more adept at cloaking their dissent. A few foreign observers remarked on Russia's "chill of fear," a sentiment that seemed to clamp down on creativity and freedom.

Prelude to the Crimean War

By the early 1850s, Nicholas's foreign policies were increasingly assertive, especially regarding the declining Ottoman Empire. Russia sought to expand influence in the Balkans and gain control over territories near the Black Sea. This alarmed Britain and France, who feared a shift in the balance of power. Diplomatic tensions escalated, eventually leading to the outbreak of the Crimean War in 1853—a conflict that would reveal the fragility of Nicholas's carefully controlled empire.

Nicholas died in 1855, during the war, having witnessed disastrous military failures that contradicted his image of Russian might. While official bulletins presented him as a steadfast leader to the end, private accounts suggest he was devastated by reports of defeats and the army's inability to match the more industrialized forces of Britain and France. His death occurred in the midst of a conflict that would shape Russia's trajectory, forcing the next generation of rulers to confront the glaring weaknesses that Nicholas's era of strict surveillance had tried so hard to conceal.

CHAPTER 12

THE CRIMEAN WAR AND ITS LASTING DAMAGE

Introduction

The mid-19th century brought Russia face-to-face with its own limitations when it clashed with Britain, France, and the Ottoman Empire in the Crimean War (1853–1856). For decades, the Russian Empire under Nicholas I had portrayed itself as a bastion of order and a savior of Christian Orthodoxy, intent on expanding influence in the Balkans and the Near East. However, the Crimean War would expose glaring flaws in Russia's military, economy, and broader social framework. What began as a geopolitical struggle over influence in the declining Ottoman Empire soon became a harrowing ordeal for Russian soldiers and civilians alike.

This chapter examines the origins of the Crimean War, key battles like the Siege of Sevastopol, and the horrific conditions endured by those on the front lines. We will explore the consequences for Russia's standing in Europe, as well as the internal shockwaves that pressed the government to reconsider its reliance on serfdom and outdated administrative practices. While the war ended in diplomatic humiliation for Russia, its deeper legacy lay in revealing how far behind the empire had fallen in terms of technology, healthcare, and social development. Indeed, the Crimean War set the stage for the transformative reforms of Alexander II, who recognized that clinging to the old order was no longer tenable.

The Road to War: Rivalries and Ambitions

Religious Tensions and the "Eastern Question"

Throughout the 19th century, the Ottoman Empire was in decline, and European powers jockeyed for influence in its territories. Russia saw itself as the protector of Orthodox Christians under Ottoman rule, frequently intervening in Balkan affairs. At the same time, Britain and France worried that Russia sought to seize control of key straits, particularly the Bosporus and the Dardanelles, which would give the empire access to the Mediterranean and disrupt the balance of power.

A series of disputes over Christian holy sites in Palestine—particularly the rights of Orthodox monks versus Catholic monks—provided a spark. When diplomatic efforts failed, Nicholas I ordered Russian troops to occupy Ottoman vassal states in the Danubian Principalities (modern-day Romania). The Ottomans declared war on Russia in October 1853, confident that they would receive support from Britain and France.

British and French Concerns

Britain feared that unchecked Russian expansion threatened vital trade routes to India. France, under Emperor Napoleon III, was keen to assert its prestige and reestablish a leading role in European politics. Both countries sided with the Ottoman Empire, dispatching naval forces to the Black Sea. By the spring of 1854, Britain and France had formally declared war on Russia. The conflict thus escalated from a localized quarrel over religious privileges into a major European confrontation, pulling in thousands of troops and enormous resources.

Early Engagements: The Danube and the Black Sea

Battles on the Danube

Russian forces initially achieved some success against the Ottomans along the Danube River. However, the entrance of British and French armies reversed Russia's momentum. Facing superior artillery and better-coordinated armies, the Russians could not easily sustain an offensive in these distant territories. Moreover, the Russian command structure showed its rigidity, stifling the initiative of local officers.

Faced with a multi-front conflict, Nicholas I looked to fortify the Black Sea region, especially the Crimean Peninsula, where the Russian naval base at Sevastopol became a focal point of defense. But this pivot would invite the combined Franco-British expedition to land in Crimea in September 1854, setting the stage for one of the war's most grueling campaigns.

Naval Clashes and Technological Disparities

While the Russian Black Sea Fleet had some formidable ships, it lagged behind the modern steam-powered vessels fielded by Britain and France. Russian naval technology remained reliant on sail-powered warships, and their coastal fortifications, though numerous, were often obsolete. The Allies, by contrast, employed steam-driven battleships and newly improved explosive shells, which devastated wooden hulls.

This technological gap manifested early in the war. A major naval showdown occurred at Sinope in November 1853, where the Russian fleet annihilated an Ottoman squadron, confirming Russia's local dominance. However, the triumph at Sinope also alarmed Britain and France, who redoubled their resolve to neutralize Russian naval power in the Black Sea. Their advanced ships would soon blockade key ports, stranding Russian squadrons and curtailing supply lines.

The Invasion of Crimea and the Siege of Sevastopol

Landing at Kalamita Bay

In September 1854, Allied forces landed near Kalamita Bay, north of Sevastopol. Comprising French, British, Ottoman, and later Sardinian troops, they marched south with the intent to capture Russia's principal naval stronghold in the region. The Russians, under Prince Menshikov, attempted to halt them at the Alma River but were outgunned and outmaneuvered. This defeat forced the Russians to retreat closer to Sevastopol, setting in motion a protracted siege.

The Hell of Sevastopol

The Siege of Sevastopol (October 1854–September 1855) became the war's defining episode. Allied troops encircled the city from land while their navy controlled the seas. Sevastopol's defenders, led by Admiral Vladimir Kornilov, Admiral Pavel Nakhimov, and other heroic figures, dug extensive fortifications and artillery positions. The Russians scuttled ships at the harbor's entrance to block enemy vessels, turning the city into a fortress.

However, conditions inside Sevastopol deteriorated rapidly. The city's civilian population had largely fled, leaving soldiers and naval personnel to endure shortages of food, clean water, medical supplies, and shelter. The Russian high command struggled to supply the garrison; poor roads and logistical chaos hampered efforts to bring in reinforcements or provisions. Soldiers huddled in trenches and tunnels while Allied artillery battered them day and night.

Allied Hardships

While often overshadowed by the Russians' misery, the Allied troops also suffered terribly. Winter in Crimea was harsher than many British or French soldiers had ever experienced. Inadequate uniforms, poor camp sanitation, and the spread of diseases like cholera and dysentery claimed thousands of lives. The infamous "Charge of the Light Brigade" at the Battle of Balaclava (October 1854) epitomized the kind of miscommunication and reckless bravery that led to needless deaths. Allied command structures, like those of the Russians, were riddled with incompetence and political rivalries.

Yet the Allies maintained their siege, bolstered by greater industrial capacity. Supplies—rifles, cannons, ammunition—arrived by sea, along with reinforcements. Engineers built roads and the first military railway in Crimea to transport heavy artillery closer to the siege lines. This contrast in logistical organization underscored the gulf between Russia's archaic systems and the more modern methods employed by the Western powers.

The Toll on Soldiers and Civilians

Disease and Suffering

Disease ravaged both sides far more than combat did. Cholera, scurvy, typhus, and dysentery flourished in the unsanitary conditions of the camps. For the Russian defenders, cramped quarters and insufficient medical care spelled disaster. Doctors lacked knowledge of modern antiseptic techniques, and field hospitals became breeding grounds for infection. Amputations were common for wounded limbs, with rudimentary pain relief.

Civilians in the Crimean Peninsula—especially those unable to flee—were caught in the middle. Villages were requisitioned for supplies, local inhabitants sometimes forced into labor for one army or the other. Winter storms and flooding destroyed harvests, contributing to famine in some areas. The war's violence disrupted trade routes across the Black Sea, harming the broader economy. In the rest of Russia, families awaited letters from sons, husbands, or fathers drafted into service, often receiving none.

Heroic Medical Efforts

Not all was grim despair; the Crimean War also witnessed pioneering medical work that saved thousands of lives. The most famous example is Florence Nightingale, the British nurse who organized sanitary practices in military hospitals and drastically reduced mortality rates. Although her direct impact on Russian casualties was minimal, her example and the work of doctors on both sides introduced new standards of wartime medicine. Over time, these lessons would influence Russian medical reforms, though Nicholas I's government took little immediate notice.

Nicholas I's Death and the Final Fall of Sevastopol

Nicholas I's Despair

As reports of military setbacks, disease outbreaks, and bureaucratic failures streamed in, Nicholas I's confidence in his autocratic system wavered. He had built his regime on the premise of Russian military might and the integrity of an all-powerful state. Now it was painfully evident that the empire's infrastructure, supply chains, and technology were outmoded. Some historians argue that Nicholas was so disheartened by the Crimean debacle that it hastened his death. He passed away on March 2, 1855 (February 18, Old Style), with rumors suggesting he succumbed either to pneumonia or to a broken spirit.

Alexander II and the Endgame

Nicholas's son, Alexander II, inherited the throne at this precarious moment. Despite limited experience, Alexander recognized that continuing the war indefinitely could devastate Russia further. Still, the siege of Sevastopol dragged on. Both sides exchanged brutal bombardments and trench assaults. The Malakhov Kurgan, a key Russian defensive position, became symbolic of the defenders' tenacity.

Ultimately, after eleven months of siege, Allied forces captured vital fortifications in September 1855. Russian troops evacuated Sevastopol, blowing up their remaining installations. The city lay in ruins, strewn with corpses and debris. Though some scattered fighting continued elsewhere, the fall of Sevastopol effectively decided the war.

The Treaty of Paris (1856): A Humiliating Peace

Diplomatic Concessions

Russia entered peace negotiations in a weakened position. The Treaty of Paris, signed on March 30, 1856, imposed harsh terms:

- Russia had to relinquish its claim to protect Orthodox Christians in the Ottoman Empire.
- The Black Sea was neutralized—no warships could be stationed there, crippling Russia's naval presence.
- The Danubian Principalities gained greater autonomy, reducing Russia's influence in the Balkans.

For a nation that prided itself on being the "Third Rome" and protector of Orthodoxy, these terms were humiliating. Russian diplomats strained to preserve some dignity, but the blow to national prestige was undeniable. The treaty also signaled a shift in the European balance of power, with Britain and France emerging as the main guardians of the Ottoman Empire's territorial integrity, at least for a time.

Domestic Fallout

The war's end brought scant relief to Russian families who had lost loved ones or property. Industries that supplied the military floundered amid the sudden cessation of large orders. Veterans returned to find few avenues for integration, as the economy could not easily absorb them. Petty bureaucrats who had grown used to war-related tasks sometimes lost their positions, fueling unemployment.

Alexander II, for his part, concluded that Russia needed profound reforms to compete with the West. He soon embarked on major initiatives—most notably the Emancipation of the Serfs in 1861—seeking to modernize the empire's social and economic foundations. While these changes fall beyond the direct scope of Nicholas I's reign, they emerged largely as a response to the failures exposed by the Crimean War.

Life During Wartime: Firsthand Horrors and Legacy

Soldiers' Letters and Memoirs

Contemporary accounts from Russian soldiers and officers paint a grim picture of the Crimean War's frontline life. Letters to relatives describe unheated dugouts in icy winters, meager rations crawling with insects, and the despair of seeing comrades succumb to disease or enemy shells. Some wrote with fatalistic resignation, convinced they would not return home. Others preserved a sense of duty, buoyed by religious faith or patriotism.

Memoires by Russian officers published after the war offer insights into command failures. Corruption, nepotism, and fear of stepping outside protocol stifled the kind of bold leadership that might have mitigated disasters. Even braver leaders—like Admiral Nakhimov, who died of a sniper's bullet—found themselves hamstrung by scarce resources and outdated tactics.

Civilian Suffering and "The Sick Man of Europe"

Civilians in Crimea recounted how entire villages were stripped bare for fodder, wagons, or conscript labor. Those living near supply routes became pawns, forced to feed armies of whichever side controlled the region at the moment. Disease spread to nearby towns, where medical infrastructure collapsed under the influx of wounded. The trauma endured by these communities lingered long after the armies departed.

In the broader European context, the war hammered home the reality that the Ottoman Empire—derisively called "the Sick Man of Europe"—was a fragile entity propped up by Western powers. For Russia, the label of "sick man" might also apply, at least metaphorically, to an autocratic system battered by the revelations of war. Even though Russia retained massive territories and resources, it lagged dangerously behind in industrialization and governance.

Consequences and the Path to Reform

Shattered Myths of Invincibility

The Crimean War shattered the myth of Russian invincibility that had been carefully cultivated during the reign of Nicholas I. No longer could Russia claim moral or military superiority over Western powers. The illusions that autocracy and rigid discipline alone would suffice in modern warfare fell apart amid the rubble of Sevastopol. The humiliations inflicted at the negotiation table reinforced this reality.

This blow to national pride created a collective soul-searching among the elite. Pamphlets circulated—sometimes clandestinely, given ongoing censorship—criticizing the bureaucracy, the stifling of innovation, and the inertia of serfdom. Many believed Russia could not hope to advance unless it undertook structural reforms. The seeds of a new era were thus planted, albeit in blood-soaked soil.

The Pivotal Role of Alexander II

Alexander II took power at a moment ripe for change. Though he inherited Nicholas I's secret police apparatus and formal devotion to autocracy, he recognized that continuing his father's approach would only invite further disaster. The Crimean War had exposed not just military failings but also economic stagnation and social unrest brewing among peasants, soldiers, and educated urbanites.

Within a few years, Alexander II enacted the Great Reforms, including the emancipation of 23 million serfs in 1861. While these reforms were partial and fraught with complications, they represented a dramatic break from the policies of Nicholas's era. The impetus came directly from the Crimean debacle, which had proven that the old systems were untenable in the face of modern statecraft and war.

CHAPTER 13

ALEXANDER II'S REFORMS AND VIOLENT RESPONSES

Introduction

The Crimean War ended in 1856 with Russia's defeat and a humbling peace. This outcome revealed serious weaknesses in the empire: its army lagged technologically behind Western powers, its infrastructure was primitive, and its economy remained overwhelmingly dependent on serf labor. When Tsar Nicholas I died in the midst of the war, his son Alexander II inherited not just a battered military, but also a nation on the brink of major change. The new emperor recognized that clinging to the old order could spell disaster if Russia ever faced another modernized enemy.

In a bold departure from his father's approach, Alexander II embarked on the most significant program of domestic reforms since Peter the Great. Foremost among these measures was the emancipation of the serfs in 1861—a momentous act that liberated over 20 million peasants. Alexander also introduced reforms to local government, the judiciary, and the military, hoping to modernize Russia along more European lines. However, these changes came with limitations, compromises, and unintended consequences. Many peasants found freedom ambiguous when saddled with redemption payments and limited land. Local assemblies (zemstvos) gave citizens a taste of self-government, but their authority was strictly limited. The judicial system grew more transparent, yet the tsar's autocratic power remained paramount.

Initially, Alexander II's reign seemed like a new dawn of liberalization. Yet the surge of hope was accompanied by unrest. Radical groups demanded faster, deeper changes. Terrorist factions emerged, carrying out bombings and assassinations to destabilize the regime. The state, under pressure from revolutionary violence, enacted repressive measures that coexisted uneasily with the earlier reforms. This chapter delves into the reforms of Alexander II, the challenges of implementing them in a vast and conservative empire, and the violent reactions—both from rebels who felt reforms did not go far enough and from government forces determined to suppress dissent.

The Aftermath of Crimea and the "Era of Great Reforms"

A Society Ripe for Change

The Crimean War had revealed the empire's economic and social backwardness. Calls for reform came from multiple corners: liberal nobles who had seen Europe's modernization firsthand, intellectuals who believed that the old feudal order stifled progress, and even pragmatic bureaucrats who recognized the urgent need to streamline administration. Alexander II, aware of the growing discontent, concluded that freeing the serfs was both a moral necessity and a strategic imperative. Without addressing the root causes of the empire's stagnation, Russia risked further defeats on the international stage.

At the same time, the tsar faced resistance from landowners and conservatives. Serf labor formed the economic backbone of many noble estates, and any talk of emancipation threatened their material interests. Court intrigues and high-level debates raged over how to manage such a sweeping transformation without provoking a social collapse—or, even worse in elite eyes, a revolution from below.

Early Steps Toward Emancipation

In 1857, Alexander formed a secret committee to study the serf question. Progress was slow, with multiple proposals debated. Some advocated immediate, unconditional freedom for all serfs; others insisted on a gradual process, ensuring that landlords received compensation. Fearing unrest if reforms were delayed too long, Alexander eventually took decisive action. On February 19, 1861 (Old Style), he signed the Emancipation Manifesto, unveiling it to the public in March.

The "Great Reform," as it came to be known, abolished the legal status of serfdom across the empire. Peasants were now "free" in the sense that they could marry without permission, own property independently, and seek employment beyond their village. Yet these gains were tempered by complex stipulations. Peasants were granted land but had to pay redemption fees to their former landlords, often over decades. In many regions, the allotted plots proved too small or of poor quality, forcing peasants to struggle under a new economic burden.

Emancipation of the Serfs: Hopes, Realities, and Disappointments

The Terms of Freedom

The Emancipation Manifesto established that landowners would receive financial compensation from the state, which in turn demanded repayment from the peasants in the form of redemption payments. Legally, peasants could not leave their communes until these payments were completed. This arrangement effectively tied many former serfs to their local "mir," a communal structure that oversaw land distribution and tax collection. While the mir offered some sense of local autonomy, it also limited individual mobility and economic initiative.

Many peasants discovered that "freedom" did not translate into prosperity. The redemption payments were steep, and local officials favored landlords in delineating how much land would be assigned to each household. Some peasants ended up with less farmland than they had access to under serfdom, making it harder to earn a living. Crop failures or personal misfortunes could push families into debt or force them into seeking seasonal labor elsewhere.

Noble Reactions and Adjustments

Landowners, for their part, often resented losing what they viewed as their traditional property—serf labor. Though they received state bonds as compensation, the sums did not always match the full economic value they had placed on the peasants' work. Furthermore, nobles unaccustomed to managing estates without coerced labor faced economic challenges of their own. Some adapted by employing wage labor, introducing modern farming techniques, or investing in nascent industries. Others fell into debt or sold off land, fueling a gradual, uneven process of social transformation.

Despite frustrations among both peasants and nobles, the end of serfdom was an irreversible milestone. Russia joined other major European states in dismantling feudal relations, albeit decades after Western Europe. Although the immediate benefits proved elusive to many, emancipation laid the groundwork for future modernization. Peasants gained a legal identity, which over time allowed some to migrate to cities and find industrial or service jobs. A portion of the nobility pivoted to commercial ventures or professional careers. Rural economies slowly diversified.

Broader Reforms: Local Self-Government, the Judiciary, and the Military

Zemstvo Reform

In 1864, Alexander II introduced local self-government bodies known as zemstvos in provincial and district levels. These councils, composed of elected representatives from the nobility, peasant communes, and towns, were tasked with managing local affairs: roads, schools, public health, and basic infrastructure. Zemstvos had limited tax-raising powers, but their creation marked a shift toward more participatory governance. For the first time, peasants (albeit indirectly) had some voice in local decisions.

However, the noble class retained a disproportionate influence within zemstvos, due to weighted voting systems favoring landowners. The central government also kept tight oversight, wary of allowing these assemblies to become hotbeds of political opposition. Despite such constraints, zemstvos gradually fostered a new class of civic-minded professionals—teachers, doctors, agricultural experts—who sought to improve the welfare of ordinary Russians. Their work in education and healthcare made a tangible difference, although they often struggled with inadequate funding and bureaucratic meddling.

Judicial Reforms

Alexander's regime also overhauled the judiciary in 1864, aiming to bring Russian legal practices closer to Western standards of fairness and transparency. The reforms introduced open court trials, the right to legal representation, and trial by jury for certain criminal cases. Judges were granted greater independence, theoretically reducing the influence of local officials or corrupt aristocrats on verdicts.

For many Russians, this was their first exposure to the idea that the law, not the whim of a landlord or official, should determine justice. Court proceedings were open to the public, allowing journalists—when censorship permitted—to report on cases. An independent bar emerged, with lawyers who gained reputations for defending peasant rights or challenging administrative abuses. Still, the reforms had limits: political offenses were often excluded from jury trials, and the state could intervene in sensitive cases. Over time, the new system faced partial rollbacks, particularly as revolutionary sentiments rose and the government grew more repressive.

Military Modernization

Acknowledging that the Crimean War had exposed the backwardness of Russia's army, Alexander II introduced military reforms in the 1860s and 1870s. One of the most significant changes was the introduction of universal military conscription in 1874, replacing a system in which serfs could be conscripted for decades while nobles often avoided service. Now all social classes, including the nobility, were ostensibly subject to the draft, although in practice wealthy families could still secure exemptions.

The reformed army shortened service terms and placed greater emphasis on professional training. Western-style military academies were established, new rifles and artillery adopted, and the railroad network expanded to enable faster troop movements. These measures improved Russia's defensive capabilities, although they also brought peasants and townspeople into close contact, facilitating the spread of new ideas—including radical ones.

Rising Discontent: Populists, Radicals, and the Seeds of Terrorism

The Intelligentsia's Shifting Goals

Despite—or perhaps because of—the "Great Reforms," a new generation of educated Russians found the pace of change too slow and the remaining autocracy too rigid. The intelligentsia, a broad group including students, writers, and professionals, drew on European socialist and anarchist theories. Many believed that Russia could leapfrog Western capitalist phases if peasants, freed from the vestiges of feudalism, embraced communal living and direct democracy.

This idealism fueled the Populist (Narodnik) movement of the 1870s, where educated youth went "to the people," attempting to mobilize peasants for political transformation. Narodniks preached an agrarian socialism, hoping to empower villages to self-organize and overthrow the tsarist regime. Yet they discovered that many peasants distrusted outsiders and clung to traditional beliefs. Police surveillance and arrests also stymied Narodnik activity.

The Turn to Violence

Frustrated by the lack of mass support, a more radical faction concluded that direct action against state symbols might spark a broader uprising. They formed secret societies that advocated terrorism as a way to strike fear into the government. One such group, known as "Land and Liberty," later split into factions like "The People's Will" (Narodnaya Volya) and "Black Repartition." The People's Will, in particular, gained notoriety for its sophisticated planning of high-profile assassinations.

The terrorists targeted officials they deemed pillars of the autocratic system—police chiefs, governors, and eventually the tsar himself. Bombings and shootings punctuated the latter half of Alexander II's reign. These violent acts, while modest in scale, shocked high society and triggered harsh police crackdowns. The radical underground, for its part, believed that each assassination would weaken the regime's resolve and potentially ignite popular revolt.

Government Repression: Secret Police and Reactionary Backlash

The Rise of the "Third Section" and Later Security Bodies

Although Nicholas I had created the Third Section secret police, Alexander II initially relaxed some surveillance. But as terror attacks mounted, the state reasserted control with new vigor. By the 1870s, a reorganized security apparatus known as the Department of State Police (later under the Ministry of Internal Affairs) expanded its network of spies and informants. Warrants for searches and arrests grew more frequent, and trials for political offenses often occurred behind closed doors.

High-ranking officials who had once supported moderate reforms shifted to reactionary stances, arguing that leniency encouraged revolutionaries. Calls for a constitution or broader civil liberties fell on deaf ears as the government insisted that the empire's stability hinged on reaffirming autocratic authority. Newspapers faced stricter censorship if they reported sympathetically on radical grievances.

Trial of the "Fifty," the "One Hundred and Ninety-Three," and Other Showcases

In the late 1870s, the regime staged large public trials of suspected revolutionaries, aiming to deter sympathizers. These high-profile proceedings, such as the "Trial of the 50" (1877) and the "Trial of the 193" (1877–1878), indicted students, intellectuals, and workers accused of conspiracy against the state. While some defendants received lengthy prison terms or exile to Siberia, others used the trials as platforms to denounce the government. Their speeches, though censored, reached segments of the public, inspiring further radicalism among disaffected youth.

The tsar's advisors hoped that showcasing the revolutionaries' guilt would rally loyal subjects. Instead, many observers were disturbed by the heavy-handed sentences and the government's reluctance to address underlying social issues. A cycle of tightening repression and intensifying radicalism emerged, each feeding the other.

The Assassination of Alexander II

Multiple Attempts on the Tsar's Life

Alexander II became the prime target for The People's Will, whose members saw him as the embodiment of autocracy—despite his earlier reforms. Between 1879 and 1881, assassins repeatedly tried to kill him. They planted bombs in the Winter Palace, sabotaged railway tracks used by the tsar's train, and ambushed his carriage. The authorities responded by doubling personal security, but leaks from sympathizers within government circles sometimes aided the conspirators.

The tsar oscillated between proposing cautious constitutional experiments and yielding to hardline advisors who demanded more crackdowns. He understood that public dissatisfaction extended beyond the radical fringe—liberal nobles and professionals also voiced the need for deeper systemic changes. Alexander even drafted a plan for a consultative assembly, but it was delayed by ongoing terrorism fears. History shows this hesitation proved fatal.

Fatal Explosion on the Streets of St. Petersburg

On March 1, 1881 (Old Style), Alexander II rode through St. Petersburg in his carriage. Terrorists from The People's Will lay in wait. A first bomb thrown at the carriage damaged it, killing bystanders and members of the escort. Against advice, the tsar stepped out to check on the wounded. A second assassin hurled another explosive, which tore through the emperor's body. Gravely injured, Alexander II was rushed to the Winter Palace, where he died soon after. This shocking act ended the life of the "Tsar-Liberator," who had freed the serfs but found himself the victim of an increasingly violent revolutionary movement.

Consequences of the Assassination

A Nation in Shock

The assassination stunned Russia. Many who criticized the regime still recoiled at the brutality of the act. Alexander II had represented a hope—however faint—for continued reform. Now that hope lay shattered alongside his mortally wounded body. Crowds gathered in hushed grief at the capital's churches, while officials scurried to tighten security measures. Portraits of the tsar-liberator adorned black-draped public squares, and newspapers carried stories praising his early reforms and lamenting the turn toward terror.

For conservatives, the murder confirmed their worst fears: any concession to liberalism only emboldened radicals. They pressed for a return to heavy-handed autocracy. For radical circles, the event was a mixed victory. They had eliminated the central figure of the state, yet the broader population did not rise in rebellion. Instead, the public mood swung toward caution, dreading further chaos.

Alexander III's Ascension and a Harsh Turn

Alexander II's son, Alexander III, came to power in an atmosphere charged with anxiety. His father's corpse lay in state, a reminder of the violent potential of revolution. Surrounded by reactionary advisors, Alexander III concluded that reform had led to instability and concluded that Russia needed firmer autocratic rule. This new tsar reversed many of his father's liberalizing policies, reasserting official nationalism and strengthening the security apparatus. Press censorship tightened, political trials became more frequent, and the era of the so-called "counter-reforms" began.

For those who had looked to Alexander II's reign as a potential turning point toward constitutional governance, the new climate was disheartening. Hopes for meaningful political participation or broader civil liberties were shelved. The cycle of underground radicalism persisted, now confronting a government determined to crush any hint of dissent.

Evaluation of Alexander II's Legacy

The Paradox of the "Tsar-Liberator"

Alexander II's reign was marked by bold transformations that freed the serfs, modernized local governance, revised the judicial system, and introduced more equitable military service. At the same time, these reforms were partial, often constrained by the tsar's desire to preserve autocracy. Peasants gained legal freedom but remained tethered to communes and saddled with debts. Local zemstvos had limited power, and the central state maintained ultimate authority. The judicial reforms did not extend to political crimes, allowing the regime to repress dissent outside normal legal channels.

Nevertheless, these measures stirred society in unprecedented ways. Former serfs began migrating to cities, fueling urban growth and a nascent industrial workforce. Emerging professionals staffed zemstvo schools and clinics, fostering new ideas about civic responsibility and social justice. Intellectuals tested the boundaries of censorship, producing literature that openly or subtly critiqued the old order.

Seeds of Future Conflict and Transformation

Alexander II's reforms created both new opportunities and new frustrations. By partially opening space for debate, they exposed deeper systemic problems. The radical intelligentsia saw half-measures as evidence that the ruling class would never relinquish true power voluntarily. Their turn to terrorism sparked a cycle of repression that ultimately led to the tsar's assassination. Conservative forces used the violence to justify a clampdown, halting much of the reform momentum.

Despite the reactionary shift following Alexander II's death, the changes he initiated could not be entirely undone. Serfdom was gone, replaced by a more fluid but still unequal social structure. The zemstvo system, though limited, continued to function and shaped local governance. The newly empowered courts remained a channel—however imperfect—for legal redress and professional legal culture. Over the coming decades, industrialization, urbanization, and the spread of literacy would accelerate, setting the stage for further upheaval.

CHAPTER 14

THE RISE OF REVOLUTIONARY IDEAS UNDER ALEXANDER III

Introduction

When Alexander II was assassinated in 1881, his son Alexander III ascended to the throne amidst an atmosphere of grief, fear, and mounting political tension. The violent death of the "Tsar-Liberator" had shocked the nation, reinforcing conservative factions' belief that liberal reforms invited anarchy. Alexander III, a physically imposing figure known for his blunt manner, vowed to restore the authority of the autocracy and suppress any hint of revolutionary sentiment. Under his reign (1881–1894), Russia witnessed a sharp turn toward reactionary policies, increased censorship, and heightened police surveillance.

Yet the forces unleashed by Alexander II's reforms could not be fully contained. Industrialization continued apace, fueled in part by the demands of the growing railway network and nascent manufacturing industries. Urban centers swelled with peasants in search of factory work, mixing with educated youth who formed the backbone of an expanding intelligentsia. Despite stricter censorship, radical literature and underground political organizations persisted, finding new ways to evade the watchful eye of the state. Meanwhile, dissatisfaction festered: ethnic minorities resented policies of Russification, factory workers endured long hours and low pay, and peasants who hoped for land struggled with debt and communal constraints.

In this chapter, we explore the contradictory currents of Alexander III's Russia. On one hand, the emperor and his ministers clamped down on free expression, targeted non-Russian communities, and tightened the screws of autocratic control. On the other hand, industrial growth and the lingering effects of earlier reforms incubated new forms of social and political consciousness. We will examine how revolutionary ideas adapted to this hostile environment—shifting from populist tactics to Marxist analysis—and how the state responded with ever more sophisticated methods of repression. This tension set the stage for the final decades of Romanov rule, as seeds of opposition took root among an increasingly diverse array of social groups.

Alexander III's Vision: Orthodoxy, Autocracy, Nationality

A Reactionary Ascension

Alexander III was crowned in 1883, but his de facto rule began in 1881 amid the immediate crisis of his father's assassination. Influenced by conservative advisors such as Konstantin Pobedonostsev (procurator of the Holy Synod) and Mikhail Katkov (a leading journalist), Alexander concluded that Russia's stability depended on reversing the liberal drift of Alexander II's later years. The new tsar perceived constitutional ideas and press freedoms as thinly veiled threats to autocracy.

Within months, Alexander III approved the "Statute on Measures for the Protection of State Security and Social Order" (1881), granting local authorities sweeping powers to declare a state of emergency. This statute allowed for arbitrary arrests, censorship, and exiling of suspects without trial. It provided the legal framework for a wave of crackdown on activists, writers, and even moderate critics. The Okhrana, a special branch of the police, gained an expanded role in infiltrating and suppressing political groups.

Reaffirming Orthodoxy and Russification

Alexander III doubled down on promoting the triad of "Orthodoxy, Autocracy, Nationality," championed since Nicholas I's reign. However, he did so more aggressively. The Orthodox Church received state backing to conduct missionary work among non-Orthodox populations, especially in border regions. Catholic or Protestant communities in the Baltic provinces, as well as Muslim populations in the Volga region and Central Asia, encountered new pressures to adopt Russian language and customs. These policies, collectively known as "Russification," sought to unify the empire under a single national identity.

For ethnic minorities such as Poles, Ukrainians, Finns, and Jews, Russification meant the erosion of local languages and cultures. In the Kingdom of Poland, Russian replaced Polish in official settings and schools. In the Baltic provinces, German or Latvian used in education was heavily restricted. The regime also enacted a series of harsh policies known as the "May Laws" against Jews (1882), limiting where they could live, what professions they could hold, and restricting educational opportunities. Pogroms—violent attacks on Jewish communities—flared up in multiple regions, often with minimal intervention by the authorities. For many minorities, these experiences fueled a sense of alienation and resentment, driving some toward radical ideologies that promised liberation from autocratic rule.

Industrial Surge and the Growth of a Working Class

Witte's Economic Policies

Despite his reactionary social stance, Alexander III recognized the strategic importance of industrial development. His reign saw the early influence of Sergei Witte, a dynamic economist who would later serve as finance minister under Nicholas II. Witte championed state-led industrialization, encouraging foreign investment and spearheading the expansion of Russia's rail networks. He believed that modern industries—especially steel, coal, and textiles—would strengthen the empire economically and militarily, making it less vulnerable to foreign threats.

The government imposed high tariffs to protect burgeoning Russian industries, built new rail lines (including the initial planning of the Trans-Siberian Railway), and offered tax breaks to foreign firms willing to invest in Russian manufacturing. These policies spurred impressive economic growth rates in the 1880s and 1890s, transforming cities like St. Petersburg, Moscow, and the Donbass region into industrial hubs. Urban populations swelled as peasants migrated for factory jobs, forging a new social stratum: the industrial proletariat.

Conditions for Factory Workers

For many workers, however, the promise of industrialization soured upon encountering the harsh realities of factory life. Low wages, long hours (often 12 to 14 hours a day), and unsafe conditions were the norm. Housing was cramped and unsanitary, with entire families or groups of single laborers packed into small rooms in rapidly built tenements. Child labor remained common, and workplace accidents were frequent.

A nascent labor movement emerged, driven by the need for self-defense against exploitative employers. Strikes, though illegal, began to occur sporadically. Workers formed mutual aid societies to pool resources for medical care or funeral costs. The state responded inconsistently: at times ignoring localized labor disputes, at other times sending police or troops to break strikes forcefully. Some factory owners recognized that stable labor relations benefited productivity, while others relied on hired thugs or police connections to intimidate and sack agitators.

Intellectual Shifts: From Populism to Marxism

Disillusionment with the Narodnik Legacy

The populist movements of the 1870s had largely failed to spark a peasant-based revolution. After harsh crackdowns, many Narodniks languished in prison, endured exile in Siberia, or fled abroad. Those who remained active recognized that the peasantry—steeped in traditional beliefs—were not easily converted to radical politics. Meanwhile, the regime's continued vigilance made rural organizing dangerous.

Some disillusioned activists turned their gaze toward the rapidly expanding industrial workforce. They observed that workers concentrated in factories could be more receptive to collective action than scattered peasants. This thinking aligned with emerging Marxist theories, which argued that the proletariat, not the peasantry, would be the leading force in overthrowing capitalism and autocracy. By the 1880s, translations of Karl Marx's works circulated clandestinely among intellectual circles in major cities.

Early Marxist Groups

One of the earliest Marxist groups in Russia was the "Emancipation of Labor" group, founded by exiled activists Georgi Plekhanov, Vera Zasulich, and others in Geneva (1883). They smuggled Marxist literature into Russia and engaged in polemics with populists who still prioritized the peasantry. Marxists contended that capitalism was quickly taking root, creating the social conditions for a class-conscious proletariat to rise against both capitalism and the tsarist state.

Inside Russia, clandestine study circles formed among students, clerks, and factory workers interested in socialism. These groups debated theoretical nuances and occasionally ventured into limited agitation within factories. Police raids were common, driving many activists underground. Yet the migration of peasants to industrial centers, combined with the harshness of working conditions, gave Marxist ideas a growing constituency. By the end of Alexander III's reign, a small but determined cadre of Marxists was laying the groundwork for what would become the Russian Social Democratic movement.

Heightened Repression and the Okhrana's Expanding Role

The Okhrana's Methods

Alexander III oversaw a substantial expansion of the Okhrana (Department for Protecting Public Security and Order), which evolved from earlier secret police agencies. Headquartered in St. Petersburg, the Okhrana maintained branches in major cities and discreetly placed informants in universities, factories, and even among court officials. Undercover agents infiltrated radical groups, sometimes acting as provocateurs to spur members into actions that would justify arrests. The Okhrana also monitored the press, theater, and literature, ensuring that no subversive content slipped past censors.

Arrests often occurred quietly, at night, with suspects disappearing into prison cells or Siberian exile. High-profile trials might be held publicly to intimidate others, but many cases proceeded through administrative means, bypassing formal courts. The specter of the secret police bred paranoia: individuals feared casual political discussions, as a fellow worker or student might be an informer. Despite these fears, revolutionary cells adapted, adopting coded language, safe houses, and elaborate conspiratorial structures.

Russification and Minority Crackdowns

While the Okhrana targeted radical movements, the broader state apparatus extended repressive policies to non-Russian populations. Pogroms against Jewish communities, which had begun sporadically under Alexander II, became more frequent and vicious in the 1880s. Though the government rarely endorsed these mobs officially, local authorities often turned a blind eye or intervened too late. Jewish families faced economic restrictions and social exclusion, driving many to emigrate—particularly to the United States—or to embrace revolutionary ideologies that promised an end to tsarist tyranny.

In the borderlands—Poland, the Baltic provinces, Ukraine, the Caucasus—officials imposed Russian language instruction in schools, replaced local administrators with Russians, and discouraged expressions of cultural identity. Resistance to Russification sometimes manifested in clandestine nationalist movements, with activists forming alliances with socialist or liberal circles in the empire's interior. Alexander III's regime thus confronted not just socialist revolutionaries, but also a patchwork of ethno-national groups seeking autonomy or independence.

Social Shifts and Quiet Opposition

The Emergence of a Professional Middle Class

Despite the government's attempts to freeze society in a conservative mold, economic growth stimulated the gradual rise of a professional middle class. Merchants, bankers, engineers, and skilled workers found opportunities in expanding industries and urban infrastructure projects. Universities produced a new generation of doctors, lawyers, and teachers. These professionals often participated in zemstvos or municipal councils (in the case of cities with limited self-government), honing administrative skills and a sense of civic duty.

This emerging middle class did not necessarily embrace radicalism. Many cherished social stability and sought incremental reforms rather than revolution. However, they also resented the aristocracy's continuing privileges, official corruption, and rigid censorship. Some lent covert support to liberal or social organizations, donated funds to publishing houses that skirted official censors, or quietly backed the fledgling labor movement. In time, these "bourgeois" elements would play an important role in shaping moderate opposition to autocracy.

Women's Education and Gender Debates

A notable development under Alexander III was the expansion of education for women, albeit within certain limits. Women's higher courses (Vysshie Zhenskie Kursy) emerged in major cities, offering young women the chance to pursue advanced studies. Although these courses lacked full university status, they produced a generation of educated women who read widely, participated in literary circles, and sometimes joined radical causes. In the conservative environment, the notion of politically active women was alarming to traditionalists, prompting further surveillance of women's study groups.

The "woman question" animated public discussion in journals and salons. Female radicals, like Vera Figner or Sofia Perovskaya (in earlier years), had demonstrated that women could lead or participate in revolutionary cells. Yet the state viewed such developments as a threat to patriarchal order. Government edicts occasionally restricted women's access to education or barred female students from forming associations without official approval.

Tensions and Violent Clashes

Labor Strikes and Government Force

In the late 1880s, sporadic factory strikes signaled the growing boldness of workers. While these strikes usually aimed at modest wage increases or safer conditions, authorities responded with force, seeing them as potential preludes to revolution. Police broke picket lines, arrested strike leaders, and sometimes collaborated with loyal factory bosses to blacklist agitators. Yet each wave of repression sharpened workers' sense of collective identity, forging small networks that would later serve as building blocks for socialist movements.

Terrorist Aftershocks

The People's Will, badly damaged by the aftermath of Alexander II's assassination, splintered into smaller cells. Some pursued assassinations of mid-level officials, though security measures around top figures of the regime made high-profile killings more difficult. Occasional bombings and shootings kept the memory of terrorism alive, but also justified the regime's heavy-handed measures. Over time, more radical activists shifted toward underground Marxist circles, seeing industrial organization as more effective than random terror. Still, the specter of bombs in the capital occasionally reemerged, a reminder that the cycle of violence had not been fully broken.

Foreign Affairs and Internal Pressures

Diplomatic Maneuvers

Alexander III maintained a cautious foreign policy, recognizing that another major conflict could strain Russia's still-recovering economy. He pursued an alliance with France, partly to counterbalance the growing influence of Germany and the Austro-Hungarian Empire. The newly forged Franco-Russian Alliance (1891–1894) had significant financial implications: French investors provided capital for Russian industrial projects, accelerating railway construction and armament production.

At the same time, tension in Central Asia loomed, where Russia's expansion met British interests. The so-called "Great Game" with Britain for influence in Asia continued under Alexander III, though less aggressively than under some of his predecessors. The tsar worried about the domestic consequences of overextending Russian forces. Balancing foreign alliances with domestic control, he aimed to keep the empire peaceful abroad so it could fortify itself at home.

The Famine of 1891–1892

One of the most catastrophic events during Alexander III's reign was the famine of 1891–1892, which struck large parts of the Volga region and beyond. Poor harvests, combined with archaic agricultural methods and local mismanagement, led to massive food shortages. The government's initial response was slow and bureaucratic. While the tsar eventually authorized relief measures, the famine claimed hundreds of thousands of lives, and survivors faced disease outbreaks like cholera.

The crisis exposed the fragility of rural Russia. Zemstvos, charitable organizations, and private individuals—including members of the emerging middle class—stepped in to distribute aid. Their role highlighted the potential for civil society to act more effectively than an autocratic bureaucracy. This realization deepened public skepticism about the state's competence. Critics argued that the regime's obsession with political control hampered efficient responses to social emergencies.

Legacy of Alexander III's Reactionary Rule

The Shaping of Future Unrest

By the time Alexander III died in 1894, Russia had undergone significant industrialization but remained hamstrung by autocratic rigidity and social tensions. The state's efforts to suppress dissent had not extinguished revolutionary sentiment; instead, these efforts channeled opposition into more clandestine and radical paths. The seeds of a broad-based social movement—combining the grievances of workers, peasants, minorities, and some disaffected nobles—were sown.

Economically, the empire stood at a crossroads: rapid industrial growth continued, but it was uneven and heavily dependent on foreign loans. Millions of peasants still lived in poverty, lacking real access to land ownership. Ethnic minorities felt marginalized by Russification. Intellectuals chafed under relentless censorship. All of these groups were potential allies for revolutionaries, who found receptive audiences among the disillusioned.

The Transition to Nicholas II

Alexander III's death brought his son, Nicholas II, to the throne. The new tsar inherited a state apparatus geared toward oppression but faced an increasingly complex social fabric. Witte's influence over economic policy would grow, pushing for further industrial expansion. At the same time, Nicholas II lacked his father's imposing presence and unwavering conviction in autocracy's success. He vacillated between reactionary instincts and occasional concessions, a pattern that would fuel instability.

In hindsight, Alexander III's unwavering stance against liberal or democratic reforms postponed any peaceful path to modernization. This left pent-up tensions that would eventually explode in the early 20th century. Revolutionary ideas, whether Marxist or nationalist, advanced despite the best efforts of the Okhrana and an intrusive bureaucracy. Indeed, the persistent crackdown served as a rallying point for disparate opposition movements, foreshadowing the upheavals that would mark Nicholas II's reign and ultimately sweep away the Romanov dynasty.

CHAPTER 15

HARDSHIPS IN FACTORIES AND FIELDS, AND THE DARK SIDE OF INDUSTRIAL GROWTH

Introduction

By the end of Alexander III's reign in 1894, Russia stood on a threshold between old and new. Autocratic power remained firmly in place, supported by conservative advisors and a robust secret police. Yet the empire's social and economic structure was undergoing rapid change. Under the influence of state-led industrialization policies, countless peasants streamed into cities to work in newly established factories. Large-scale enterprises—textile mills, iron foundries, rail works—offered wages and a semblance of opportunity, but they also imposed harsh working conditions that shocked many of these newcomers. Meanwhile, those who stayed in the countryside continued to face poverty, restricted land access, and communal obligations that made progress elusive.

In this chapter, we focus on the hardships endured by ordinary Russians at the turn of the 20th century, both in burgeoning industrial centers and in rural villages. We examine how the industrial boom, often hailed by officials as a sign of national progress, concealed grim realities such as child labor, low wages, workplace accidents, and suffocating urban slums. We also explore the continuing plight of peasants, who wrestled with oppressive land arrangements, periodic famine, and crippling taxes. As Russia's social fabric stretched to accommodate modern factories and railways, tensions ran high. Discontented workers and peasants found themselves seeking new avenues of protest and radical ideas, sowing the seeds of upheaval that would soon shake the empire to its core.

The Continuing Drive to Industrialize

Nicholas II and the Legacy of State-Led Growth

When Alexander III died in 1894, his son Nicholas II took the throne. Though Nicholas lacked his father's towering presence, he inherited a government apparatus still committed to economic modernization. Influential figures like Sergei Witte, who served as Minister of Finance (1892–1903), championed an even more aggressive approach to industrial expansion. Witte believed that building a robust industrial sector was essential for Russia's military and economic security. The state continued to levy high protective tariffs, welcome foreign capital, and invest heavily in railroads—most famously the Trans-Siberian Railway, which promised to unlock the empire's vast interior.

This strategy did, in fact, bring impressive economic growth in certain sectors. Rail mileage soared, and production of coal, iron, and steel rose rapidly. Cities like St. Petersburg, Moscow, Kiev, and Baku grew into major industrial hubs. Foreign investors—chiefly from France, Germany, and Britain—provided large infusions of capital. By statistical measures alone, Russia's economy was modernizing at a rapid pace. Yet these raw figures masked a host of social ills that accompanied unregulated factory work and urban overcrowding.

Concentration of Industry and Social Pressures

Unlike some Western European countries, where industrial development had progressed gradually over decades, Russia experienced a relatively compressed industrial boom. Factories employing thousands of workers appeared almost overnight. This rapid expansion meant that urban infrastructure—housing, sanitation, policing—could not keep up. Rents skyrocketed in burgeoning factory towns, forcing laborers to crowd into cramped, unsanitary quarters. Diseases like cholera, typhus, and tuberculosis spread easily in these conditions, contributing to alarmingly high mortality rates among the working class.

At the same time, the influx of ex-peasants disrupted traditional social structures. Many rural migrants struggled to adapt to the rhythms of factory life, with its strict time schedules and harsh discipline. Foremen or managers enforced production targets with fines or beatings. Corruption and bribery were commonplace in some enterprises, undermining attempts at fair labor practices. The Tsarist bureaucracy offered sporadic oversight, but local officials often colluded with factory owners or simply lacked the resources to enforce regulations. Workers felt alienated from a state that seemed more interested in economic output than in their welfare.

Factory Workers: Exploitation and Resilience

Long Hours and Meager Wages

A typical factory shift in late 19th-century Russia could last 12–14 hours, six days a week. Even on Sunday, some workers were obliged to carry out partial shifts or maintenance tasks. Overtime, if acknowledged at all, might pay a negligible rate. Many factories organized production in a way that demanded constant, repetitive motion. Supervisors walked the shop floors, quick to punish anyone who paused for rest or engaged in conversation.

Wages varied by region and occupation, but they were almost universally low. Skilled metalworkers or technicians might earn enough to feed a family, but unskilled laborers, including many women and children, lived on the brink of starvation. Some unscrupulous employers paid workers in scrip redeemable only at company-owned stores, which charged inflated prices for basic goods. Under such arrangements, laborers found themselves perpetually indebted, reliant on the factory not just for employment but for everyday necessities.

Child Labor and Its Toll

Although laws against child labor were debated, enforcement was patchy at best. Children as young as eight or nine toiled in textile mills, mines, and workshops. They often performed tasks requiring small hands—threading bobbins, clearing debris, feeding machines—while inhaling dust, chemical fumes, or coal soot. Exhaustion and malnutrition were common, and schooling was rarely an option. The state's minimal restrictions on child labor did little to protect these young workers, particularly when desperate parents needed every possible wage earner to survive.

Accidents involving children were disturbingly frequent. Unshielded machinery could entangle small limbs, causing serious injuries or amputations. Medical care was usually rudimentary, and factories sometimes dismissed injured children to avoid paying compensation. The human cost was staggering, yet official reports often understated the scale of the problem, focusing instead on production statistics that highlighted Russia's rise as an industrial power.

Solidarity and Early Worker Organizations

Despite the oppressive environment, factory workers gradually learned to band together. Mutual aid societies, formed under the guise of providing funeral expenses or emergency loans, served as early platforms for collective action. Workers who shared living quarters or ethnic backgrounds developed bonds of solidarity, looking after each other in times of illness or wage disputes.

While Nicholas II's regime frowned upon formal labor unions, clandestine groups did emerge. Inspired by Marxist or populist literature, they circulated pamphlets calling for better wages, shorter hours, and safer conditions. Increasingly, when owners refused to negotiate, workers resorted to strikes. These strikes were rarely organized on a mass scale in the 1890s—since police crackdowns were swift—but they foreshadowed a more assertive labor movement that would gain momentum in the early 20th century.

Life in the Countryside: Stagnation and Famine

The Burden of Redemption Payments

Even decades after the 1861 Emancipation, peasants continued to grapple with financial obligations to former landlords. Redemption payments—meant to compensate landowners for the "loss" of serf labor—remained a crushing weight. Although these were officially reduced or restructured in some regions, the cumulative debt still restricted peasant mobility and dampened any potential for agricultural innovation.

In many villages, land parcels were too small or too scattered for efficient farming. Communal rotation of fields, a vestige of serf-era customs, made it hard for individual families to invest in new techniques or better equipment. Crop failures from poor weather or pests could plunge entire communes into desperate hunger. The state's tax collection machinery, however, rarely paused. Even as peasants faced food shortages, they had to pay various levies—on land, livestock, and even salt or vodka.

Primitive Farming Techniques and Lack of Infrastructure

Russia's vast rural stretches lagged far behind Western Europe in agricultural modernization. Wooden ploughs and sickles were still common; few peasants owned draft animals beyond a single horse or an ox. Chemical fertilizers or mechanized harvesters existed mainly in the imaginations of progressive thinkers, rarely in actual fields. Distribution of new seeds or improved livestock breeding was sporadic, often limited to model farms operated by the nobility or by experimental zemstvos.

The limited rural infrastructure hampered access to markets. Poorly maintained dirt roads became impassable in the rainy season, isolating villages. Rail lines snaked across the empire, but local spur connections to small farming communities were scarce. Peasants who did manage to produce a surplus found it difficult to transport goods. Middlemen and local merchants often took advantage, buying grain at depressed prices and reselling it at higher urban rates. This cycle left peasants perpetually short-changed, fueling a sense of injustice.

Periodic Crises: Famine and Disease

The best-known crisis of Nicholas II's early reign was the famine of 1891–1892, which had actually begun under Alexander III. However, smaller-scale famines recurred, partly due to Russia's volatile climate and partly because of systemic inefficiencies. When harvests failed, starving peasants sometimes resorted to eating seeds meant for the next planting. Diseases like cholera or typhus would then sweep through malnourished populations, exacerbating the tragedy.

Relief efforts varied. Zemstvos, local charities, and even philanthropic nobles attempted to distribute grain or set up soup kitchens. But these endeavors were undermined by corruption, logistical failures, and the government's reluctance to acknowledge the full extent of crises. Some radical activists braved police suspicion to organize relief efforts, using them as opportunities to agitate against the regime. For many peasants, each famine underscored the state's failure to protect its most vulnerable subjects, deepening resentment that simmered just below the surface.

The Impact of Rapid Urban Growth on Families

Overcrowded Tenements and Disease

As peasants migrated to industrial centers, entire families would cram into single rooms in multi-story tenements hastily built by speculators. In cities like St. Petersburg and Moscow, these buildings became notorious for their unsanitary conditions. Contaminated water supplies, inadequate sewage, and poor ventilation bred cholera, typhus, and tuberculosis. Infant mortality soared, and life expectancy among the working class remained alarmingly low.

Officials sometimes launched clean-up drives, demolishing a few slums or establishing public bathhouses. However, without systemic housing policies or modern sanitation infrastructure, the core issues persisted. Children played in alleyways filled with garbage; adults had limited access to medical care beyond expensive private clinics or overcrowded charitable hospitals. Periodic epidemics shut down factories and overwhelmed local morgues.

Women's Roles and the Double Burden

Both in factories and at home, women bore a heavy load. Many toiled in textile mills or garment workshops, often earning significantly lower wages than men for similar tasks. They also shouldered primary responsibility for cooking, cleaning, and child-rearing. In families where the father spent long hours at work—or fell prey to alcoholism, a frequent scourge—women became the main providers and caretakers. Single mothers or widows faced an especially precarious existence, with limited support from either the state or charitable institutions.

Moreover, sexual harassment and exploitation were rife. Foremen or managers sometimes demanded sexual favors in exchange for job security or to avoid wage deductions. Social stigma discouraged victims from speaking out, and the police were unlikely to intervene unless violence escalated to murder or severe assault. While a handful of women's advocacy groups emerged, they lacked official recognition or resources to fight widespread discrimination. Many women found themselves trapped in a cycle of poverty, working themselves to exhaustion in factories only to return to substandard living conditions that further eroded their health.

Growing Discontent and Underground Agitation

Marxist Circles in the Factories

By the late 1890s, Marxist ideas had spread beyond small intellectual circles and into factory communities. Young activists, sometimes students from universities, took jobs in large industrial complexes to meet workers firsthand. They organized reading groups, taught basic literacy, and explained the concept of class struggle. Although the Okhrana constantly hunted these agitators, arresting or exiling many, a new generation of workers became politicized.

Small strikes began to erupt over wage cuts or the dismissal of popular foremen. Though modest in scope, these actions reflected a deeper shift: laborers were starting to see themselves not just as individuals locked in a survival battle, but as part of a working-class collective. Marxist cells encouraged them to link immediate demands—higher pay, shorter hours—to the ultimate goal of ending tsarist oppression and establishing a socialist society. For the Tsarist regime, this development signaled a new level of danger, as the once-unorganized masses gradually acquired a coherent ideology and network of support.

Revolutionary Leaflets and Illegal Presses

Despite censorship, underground presses proliferated, producing newspapers, pamphlets, and manifestos that were distributed in secret. Revolutionary groups devised intricate methods: hidden compartments in train cars, codes to alert contacts in different cities, and nighttime deliveries to factory dormitories. Leaflets might be read aloud to illiterate colleagues, spreading ideas by word of mouth. The authorities responded with raids, seizing printing equipment and jailing suspected editors. But for each press shut down, another seemed to spring up, sometimes in a different district or even a neighboring province.

These revolutionary writings were often short, focusing on labor issues, government corruption, or the hypocrisy of the aristocracy. Some publications included scathing critiques of the church's complicity with the autocracy. Others reported on worker strikes in Western Europe, suggesting that Russian laborers could follow the same path. The very act of reading such materials was subversive—an invitation to imagine a Russia without tsars, landlords, or exploitative factory owners.

State Reaction and Mounting Tensions

Sporadic Reforms and Inconsistent Enforcement

The Tsarist government occasionally attempted to placate discontent with partial labor legislation. Laws were enacted to reduce work hours for women and children, impose minimal safety standards, or require factory inspections. Yet these reforms were seldom enforced rigorously. Factory inspectors were too few, often corrupt or hamstrung by local officials who sided with powerful industrialists. Workers quickly learned that official edicts did not necessarily change daily life.

In rural areas, the government introduced piecemeal adjustments to land tenure or reduced certain taxes. These measures aimed to ease unrest, but they rarely addressed core structural problems—tiny plots, communal inefficiencies, and the lack of capital for improvements. Wealthy nobles often used local influence to sabotage or delay reforms that threatened their estates. Peasants, meanwhile, saw little improvement in living conditions. Many concluded that the Tsar's proclamations were either hollow gestures or cunning tactics to divert attention from deeper injustices.

Harsh Policing and Exile

As radical sentiments grew among workers and peasants, the state resorted to more intense crackdowns. The Okhrana expanded its ranks, employing undercover agents in factories to identify ringleaders. Intelligence operations targeted not just revolutionaries but also moderate zemstvo activists or liberal intellectuals. Thousands of individuals found themselves arrested on vague charges like "sedition" or "anti-state activities" and were whisked away to prisons or remote exile settlements in Siberia.

Exile, whether administrative or judicial, was a favored method for neutralizing dissidents without the spectacle of public trials. Men and women deemed politically dangerous were dispatched to harsh climates with limited means of livelihood. Despite these punitive measures, some exiles continued to write, correspond with underground networks, or eventually escape. Siberian exile villages, ironically, became hubs of political discourse where Marxists, populists, and nationalists cross-pollinated ideas.

Underlying Forces Poised to Explode

A Convergence of Grievances

By the dawn of the 20th century, Russia was a cauldron of pent-up anger. Workers in urban centers resented exploitative conditions and the gulf between their labor and their meager compensation. Peasants in countless villages still dreamed of owning sufficient land to support their families without crippling debt. Ethnic minorities chafed under Russification and religious constraints. Intellectuals and students seethed at the stagnation enforced by censorship and the lack of meaningful political participation. Although these groups differed in their specific aims, they shared a common sense of betrayal by an autocracy that demanded loyalty but offered little in return.

Rumblings of Change

While outwardly the empire's police and bureaucracy maintained an iron grip, cracks were clearly forming. Discontented laborers organized more frequent strikes, culminating in city-wide stoppages that demanded negotiation. Rural unrest took shape as occasional riots against local landlords or tax collectors. National minorities quietly consolidated their underground movements, sometimes connecting with socialist organizations that promised greater autonomy or independence. And across these diverse fronts, radical literature continued to flourish in secret, imagining a future freed from tsarist oppression.

As industrialization advanced and political ideas spread, more and more Russians recognized that the conditions they endured were not inevitable. They saw alternative models in Western Europe, where labor unions and parliaments had gained some influence. Even if they lacked a clear blueprint, they felt that change was necessary—and possibly imminent. The monarchy's reluctance to grant concessions, combined with the raw memories of state brutality, made compromise increasingly unlikely.

CHAPTER 16

THE RUSSO-JAPANESE WAR AND THE BLOODY SUNDAY TRAGEDY

Introduction

By the early 20th century, Russia's social and economic challenges were becoming more acute. Factories had multiplied, bringing throngs of peasants to overcrowded cities. Workers organized in small but growing movements, demanding better wages and conditions. Rural hardships continued, and hunger still haunted the countryside. Amid these internal strains, Tsar Nicholas II and his advisors turned their gaze toward foreign policy, hoping that imperial expansion might secure resources, enhance prestige, and distract the population from domestic troubles.

This chapter delves into Russia's ill-fated venture in the Far East, culminating in the Russo-Japanese War (1904–1905). Meant to assert Russian dominance in Asia, this conflict instead revealed deep weaknesses in the empire's military and governance. Defeat at the hands of Japan shocked both the ruling elite and ordinary Russians. Popular anger at mismanagement and corruption boiled over in early 1905, when peaceful demonstrators in St. Petersburg marched to petition the tsar—only to face gunfire from imperial troops. This "Bloody Sunday" massacre shattered the image of Nicholas II as a caring "little father" to his people, igniting nationwide unrest. Together, these events helped set the stage for the first Russian Revolution and a new era of instability.

The Road to War in the Far East

Russia's Far Eastern Ambitions

Since the mid-19th century, Russia had steadily expanded into Siberia and the Pacific coast, eager to establish warm-water ports and exploit the region's resources. Following the construction of the Trans-Siberian Railway, completed in large segments by 1903, officials in St. Petersburg believed they could rapidly deploy troops and settlers into Manchuria, Korea, and beyond. Some saw an opportunity to emulate Western powers that had claimed colonies across Asia and Africa.

Nicholas II and his foreign minister, Count Vladimir Lamsdorf, viewed Japan—a newly industrialized and militarily capable island nation—as a direct rival for influence in Korea and Manchuria. Tensions over control of these territories mounted, with both sides negotiating on and off but never reaching a stable compromise. Key advisors around the tsar, including figures in the military high command, underestimated Japan's resolve and modern weaponry. Many aristocrats believed victory would be quick and decisive, bolstering Russia's status as a great power.

Japan's Rapid Modernization

Japan, for its part, had embarked on the Meiji Restoration since 1868, transforming its feudal system into a modern state. Under Emperor Meiji, Japan developed railways, industries, and a disciplined army and navy trained by Western specialists. Victorious in the First Sino-Japanese War (1894–1895), Japan established itself as a dominant force in East Asia. Its leaders, wary of Russia's encroachment on Chinese territory and especially in Korea, prepared for confrontation.

By 1903, Japanese diplomats sought a settlement that would acknowledge Japan's special interests in Korea while granting Russia influence in Manchuria. But Russian negotiators stalled, hoping to maintain a free hand in both regions. Tensions escalated further as Russian troops occupied key positions in Manchuria, refusing to withdraw despite prior promises. In Japan's eyes, war became a means to protect its growing power and ensure a foothold in the continent.

Outbreak of the Russo-Japanese War

A Surprise Attack at Port Arthur

In February 1904, without a formal declaration of war, the Japanese navy launched a sudden assault on Russia's Pacific Fleet stationed at Port Arthur (now Lüshunkou) on the Liaodong Peninsula. Taking advantage of darkness and unprepared Russian defenses, Japanese torpedo boats inflicted serious damage on battleships and cruisers. The shock was immediate. News reached St. Petersburg that the empire was at war with a nation many considered inferior—yet already demonstrating military superiority.

Russian forces in Manchuria, lacking coordination and suffering from logistical shortfalls, struggled to respond effectively. The Trans-Siberian Railway—still not fully complete with a double track in key stretches—could not supply reinforcements quickly enough. Even as additional troops were dispatched from European Russia, they endured a grueling journey of weeks or months. Meanwhile, Japan swiftly moved armies into Korea and Manchuria, seizing strategic points and cutting off Russian garrisons.

Battles on Land and Sea

Throughout 1904 and into early 1905, a series of engagements revealed the Russian military's unpreparedness. At the Battle of Liaoyang in August 1904, Japanese forces, though numerically smaller, outmaneuvered the Russians. The fall of Port Arthur in January 1905 after a protracted siege was a devastating blow to Russian pride. The fortress, once hailed as impregnable, surrendered after months of intense bombardment and trench warfare. Thousands of Russian defenders, beset by disease and short on supplies, capitulated to the Japanese.

Russia's Baltic Fleet, renamed the Second Pacific Squadron, embarked on a desperate voyage around Africa to relieve Port Arthur. By the time it arrived in the Tsushima Strait in May 1905, Port Arthur had already fallen, and Japanese naval forces were poised for action. The ensuing Battle of Tsushima (May 27–28) ended in a catastrophic Russian defeat. Japan's modern battleships and well-trained crews decimated the exhausted Russian vessels. Over two-thirds of the Russian fleet was sunk or captured, marking one of the most lopsided naval engagements in modern history.

Domestic Repercussions: Anger and Despair

Growing Opposition to the War

As reports of defeats piled up, the Russian public grew increasingly critical of the government's conduct of war. Newspapers, despite censorship, published bleak accounts of battlefield failures and the staggering costs in lives and treasury. Families received news of sons killed or missing, often with no official explanation. Soldiers writing letters from the front described chronic shortages of ammunition, medical supplies, and even food. Morale plummeted both among troops and in the civilian population.

Political factions seized on the war as evidence of the autocracy's incompetence. Liberal zemstvo leaders, who had long campaigned for a constitution, argued that a more representative government could have avoided such a reckless conflict. Socialists, including Marxist groups, saw the war as a capitalist-imperialist venture that drained resources while workers and peasants starved. National minorities, already resentful of Russification, felt little loyalty to a regime that demanded military service for a war in distant Asia.

Economic Strains and Inflation

The war effort strained Russia's economy. Railway capacity diverted to troop and supply transport, leaving less room for commercial goods and raw materials. Factories producing munitions and military equipment scrambled to meet quotas, often imposing brutal work hours and intensifying safety hazards. Prices for staple goods soared, partly due to disruptions in grain exports and official mismanagement of distribution. Urban workers saw their wages eroded by inflation, fueling labor unrest.

Rural areas fared little better. Conscription removed young men from villages, reducing the agricultural workforce and threatening harvests. Land taxes and redemption payments remained in place, with little relief from the government. Some peasants faced hunger, while local administrators demanded they contribute grain to feed the army. Discontent brewed in the countryside, though it lacked a clear outlet beyond sporadic riots or refusal to pay taxes.

The Prelude to Bloody Sunday

Nicholas II's Isolated Court

Despite unfolding disasters in the Far East, Tsar Nicholas II remained largely insulated by his advisors and family. Residing in opulent palaces outside St. Petersburg, he received carefully curated reports that downplayed the severity of the war's failures. Ministers of the interior, the army, and finance jockeyed for influence, often contradicting each other's assessments. Some pleaded for negotiations with Japan, while others promised that new offensives could turn the tide. The tsar, indecisive and deeply religious, prayed for divine intervention but offered little direction.

As domestic unrest escalated, Nicholas II failed to grasp the depth of popular anger. He occasionally expressed concern about the plight of his "loyal subjects," but he believed in the sanctity of autocracy, guided by God's will. Calls for reforms—such as establishing an elected Duma (parliament)—fell on deaf ears. His wife, Empress Alexandra, urged Nicholas to maintain a firm hand against "subversive elements," convinced that any concession would undermine the monarchy.

Workers' Petitions and Father Gapon

By late 1904, industrial strikes had spread across St. Petersburg, driven by inflation, wage cuts, and a sense of injustice over the war. In December, a group of workers formed an Assembly under the leadership of an Orthodox priest, Father Georgy Gapon. The assembly aimed to lobby the tsar directly, hoping that he would intervene on behalf of the oppressed. Father Gapon, a charismatic figure, assured workers that Nicholas II, if properly informed, would treat their petitions with compassion.

In early January 1905, tensions peaked when management at the massive Putilov Ironworks dismissed several workers involved in protest activities. The workforce responded with strikes, and thousands more joined from other factories. Father Gapon organized a peaceful march to the Winter Palace, planning to present a petition that demanded higher wages, an eight-hour workday, and the convening of a popular assembly. The movement gained momentum swiftly, with families preparing to walk together, carrying icons and portraits of the tsar—symbols of loyalty despite their grievances.

The Bloody Sunday Massacre

A Peaceful March Meets Force

On Sunday, January 9, 1905 (January 22, New Style), tens of thousands of unarmed workers, accompanied by women and children, converged on central St. Petersburg. Singing hymns and national anthems, they hoped to demonstrate their devotion while pleading for help. Father Gapon led one of the columns, holding a cross aloft. Instead of meeting a benevolent monarch, however, they found ranks of soldiers and police blocking streets around the Winter Palace.

Nicholas II, advised of the march, had departed the city. Palace officials, fearing a revolutionary uprising, ordered troops to bar the demonstrators' path. As the crowd pressed forward, confusion reigned. Shots rang out. Some eyewitnesses claimed the troops fired warning volleys; others said they shot directly into the crowd. Panicked men, women, and children fled, trampling each other. On multiple streets, cavalry units charged into the throng, slashing with sabers. By the day's end, estimates of the dead varied from a few dozen to hundreds; many more were injured.

Public Outrage and International Shock

The massacre stunned Russia. For centuries, peasants and workers had viewed the tsar as a near-mythical guardian. The sight of them being shot while carrying icons and appeals for relief shattered that image. Newspapers—both Russian and foreign—called it "Bloody Sunday." Even conservative commentators expressed horror at the regime's brutality. Strikes erupted in major cities; peasant uprisings flared in some rural regions. Radical groups seized the moment to denounce the monarchy as irredeemably oppressive.

International reactions ranged from condemnation in liberal Western press outlets to alarm among foreign investors, who saw instability threatening their ventures in Russia. Socialist leaders across Europe condemned Nicholas II as a tyrant, praising Russian workers for their courage. The tsar's prestige plummeted. Distracted by the ongoing war with Japan, the court struggled to respond effectively to domestic fury. Father Gapon, who narrowly escaped death that day, famously lamented: "There is no God any longer. There is no Tsar." His words reverberated among a population now disillusioned with the myth of a benevolent autocrat.

The Immediate Aftermath: Unrest Spreads

Wave of Strikes and Political Turmoil

Bloody Sunday ignited a wave of strikes that paralyzed St. Petersburg and spread to industrial hubs like Moscow, Riga, Warsaw, and beyond. Workers demanded not only higher pay but also political rights—freedom of speech, assembly, and an elected parliament. Student demonstrations erupted at universities, and professors joined calls for academic freedom. Liberal zemstvo leaders convened meetings, drafting petitions that insisted on a constitution to guarantee civil liberties.

In the countryside, news of the massacre fueled peasant revolts against local landlords and tax collectors. Some villages formed self-defense units, refusing to pay levies. Others burned manor houses or seized livestock. Ethnic minority regions, already seething under Russification, seized the moment to press for autonomy or cultural rights. The empire's vast mosaic of discontents coalesced into a broader revolutionary movement that spanned class, ethnic, and regional lines.

Government's Flailing Response

Nicholas II and his ministers lurched between repression and half-hearted concessions. On one hand, the police and army cracked down hard on strikers in some cities, arresting agitators and outlawing public gatherings. On the other, the tsar promised vague reforms—such as establishing a consultative assembly—hoping to placate moderate liberals. These half-measures satisfied few. As the year wore on, radical voices gained ground, calling for outright revolution rather than incremental changes.

Mistrust between the regime and its subjects intensified. Each day, new pamphlets circulated describing the cruelty of the authorities. The war with Japan raged on, draining resources and morale. Rumors of military mutinies surfaced, with some regiments rumored to be disaffected by poor conditions and propaganda from socialist groups. The seeds of the 1905 Revolution, planted by long-standing social grievances, now germinated rapidly in the blood-soaked soil of Bloody Sunday.

The End of the War and the Lessons Learned (or Unlearned)

Negotiating Peace with Japan

By mid-1905, the Russian government, overwhelmed by domestic unrest, sought a diplomatic exit from the Far Eastern debacle. US President Theodore Roosevelt offered to mediate. The Treaty of Portsmouth, signed in September 1905, ceded control of Port Arthur and parts of southern Manchuria to Japan. Russia also recognized Japan's dominance in Korea. Although Tsarist diplomats tried to salvage face, the outcome was widely seen as a humiliating defeat—confirming that the once-mighty Russian Empire had been bested by a smaller, rapidly modernizing nation.

For Russian officers and officials, the war's end provided little relief. Soldiers returning home encountered a country in the throes of revolution. Army units, battered and resentful, became a wild card in the evolving crisis. Some remained loyal to the tsar, but others sympathized with the strikers or harbored deep cynicism toward their superiors. The illusions of a glorious campaign in the Far East were replaced by the stark reality of a wounded empire, teetering on the brink of collapse.

Intensified Revolutionary Fervor

If the Russo-Japanese War had begun as a gamble to bolster Russia's standing abroad, it ended by igniting an inferno of dissent at home. The humiliations of battlefield and diplomatic tables combined with the trauma of Bloody Sunday to awaken a broader swath of the population. Once-isolated pockets of revolutionary sentiment now found an audience in factories, barracks, and peasant communes. Political consciousness surged among ordinary people, many of whom recognized, perhaps for the first time, the power of collective action against a faltering regime.

Nicholas II's personal prestige never fully recovered. Even members of the nobility privately questioned the monarchy's direction and competence. While some reactionary aristocrats rallied around the tsar in fear of a full-scale social upheaval, others quietly leaned toward moderate reforms to stave off chaos. In effect, 1905 became a turning point, laying bare the fragility of the autocracy and foreshadowing battles yet to come.

CHAPTER 17

THE ROLE OF SECRET POLICE AND THE SHADOW OF EXILE

Introduction

In the wake of the Russo-Japanese War and the traumatic events of Bloody Sunday, Russia descended into a period of profound turmoil. Strikes, peasant uprisings, and army mutinies rattled the very foundations of the Romanov autocracy. Fearing the spread of revolution, Tsar Nicholas II and his ministers turned increasingly to the empire's secret police apparatus for salvation. The Okhrana, already formidable, expanded its operations, infiltrating factories, universities, and political groups. Spies and informants multiplied, fueling paranoia among both dissidents and ordinary citizens.

This chapter explores how the Tsarist regime wielded the secret police to suppress opposition, while also relying on the practice of exile—often to the frozen wastes of Siberia—to silence or isolate perceived enemies. We will see how these methods affected not only hardened revolutionaries but also moderate reformers, intellectuals, and members of minority communities who fell under suspicion. Despite harsh measures, the government found that oppression sometimes backfired, galvanizing those it sought to subdue. Exiled radicals used remote settlements as incubators of revolutionary theory, forging alliances that would prove critical to Russia's eventual seismic shifts. Meanwhile, the Okhrana's power to arrest, torture, and surveil stoked public resentment, contributing to a climate of fear and resistance that would again erupt in dramatic fashion.

The Okhrana's Origins and Expansion

Evolution from the Third Section

Russia's system of political policing dated back to Nicholas I's creation of the Third Section in 1826. That bureau had spied on intellectuals, nobles, and conspirators in the decades following the Decembrist Revolt. Under Alexander II, a shift occurred toward the "Department of State Police," often referred to as the Okhrana. Initially small, this agency gained prominence during the terror campaigns of the 1870s, when groups like "The People's Will" targeted high officials and eventually assassinated Alexander II himself in 1881.

Alexander III and Nicholas II further expanded the Okhrana in response to growing revolutionary activity. By the early 1900s, this secret police organization operated branches across major cities—including Warsaw, Kiev, Riga, and Tiflis—where local populations had strong nationalist or socialist movements. The Okhrana was notorious for deploying undercover agents among factory workers and student groups, trying to sniff out subversive talk. They also cultivated "agent provocateurs," who infiltrated radical cells and sometimes incited them to violent acts, thus providing a pretext for mass arrests.

Tools of Repression

The Okhrana wielded broad powers: it could conduct warrantless searches, confiscate printing presses, intercept mail, and detain suspects indefinitely without trial. Officers maintained extensive card catalogs listing thousands of "politically unreliable" individuals. Informers were everywhere—in workplaces, taverns, and even private apartments. Some agents, disguised as friendly radicals, rose to positions of trust in underground organizations, betraying entire networks when the moment seemed ripe.

Interrogations often involved threats, psychological pressure, or beatings. Though less systematized than in the later Soviet era, torture did occur, especially in remote police stations where officials felt unrestrained. Detainees might be exiled administratively—that is, without a formal court sentence—or sent to prison for months or years awaiting trial. In some notorious cases, higher officials pressured judges to deliver guilty verdicts based on Okhrana reports alone.

The Mechanics of Exile

Administrative vs. Judicial Exile

Exile functioned as a key weapon in the Tsarist arsenal. In theory, the law distinguished between "judicial exile," imposed by a court verdict after due process, and "administrative exile," decreed by government decree with minimal legal proceedings. The latter allowed officials to banish individuals deemed "undesirable" even if no concrete crime could be proven. This practice circumvented the need for public trials, thus avoiding the risk of acquittals or sympathetic jurors.

Those exiled administratively often had little warning. Police might arrive at a suspect's home in the night, present a typed order for banishment, and give them a few hours to pack. Families were sometimes allowed to accompany the exile if they chose, but that meant uprooting children and spouses, leaving behind property, jobs, and social connections. In remote Siberian towns or villages, exiles lived under periodic supervision by local authorities, restricted in their ability to move or communicate.

Life in Siberian Settlements

For many, the word "Siberia" evoked images of polar cold and desolation. In reality, Siberia was vast, with varied climates and communities. However, exiles placed in underdeveloped areas—lacking roads, schools, or decent housing—faced extreme hardships. Some endured blistering winters in wooden huts with leaky roofs, while short summers brought swarms of mosquitoes. Food supplies were erratic; exiles had to depend on small stipends from the state or wages from local labor.

Yet, exile could also become a crucible of revolutionary camaraderie. In certain districts, large numbers of exiles formed communities, sharing resources and ideas. They read forbidden literature smuggled in by sympathizers, debated strategy, and planned future actions. Some engaged in teaching local peasants, establishing makeshift schools. Over time, these exiled radicals forged alliances across ideological lines—Populists, Marxists, nationalists—united by a common enemy in the autocracy. Paradoxically, the state's desire to isolate them sometimes facilitated deeper collaboration.

High-Profile Cases and Public Awareness

The Lena Goldfields Massacre and Its Shockwaves

While the Lena Goldfields incident (1912) postdates the initial 1905 upheavals, it illustrates how the regime's repressive apparatus continued to function. Workers in Siberia's gold mines struck against appalling conditions. The management, backed by local police and Okhrana reports labeling the strikers as radicals, responded with violence. Dozens of miners were gunned down in what became known as the Lena Massacre. News of this event spread rapidly, stoking outrage and further discrediting the Tsarist regime's claims of maintaining "law and order."

Although this incident occurred a few years after the main focus of this chapter, it underscores the ongoing role of state force in suppressing labor unrest. The secret police's infiltration of mining communities likely contributed to the management's harsh response, seeing every protest as part of a grand revolutionary plot. The public's reaction—mass demonstrations in major cities—showed that, by the 1910s, Russians were increasingly aware of and angered by the regime's brutality in distant corners of the empire.

Intellectuals and the Exile of Writers

Repression did not target only explicit revolutionaries. Intellectuals who published critiques of the government, the church, or social norms risked exile or heavy fines. Writers like Maxim Gorky, who portrayed the plight of the poor and railed against hypocrisy, found themselves under constant surveillance. Another notable figure, Vladimir Korolenko, endured repeated exiles for his outspoken commentary. Such actions became known to the public through partially censored news reports and smuggled letters, casting the state in a dark light, ironically enhancing the writer's reputation among sympathetic readers.

These exiles had cultural impact. Instead of silencing dissent, the forced removal of prominent authors often elevated their status to that of folk heroes. Underground circles devoured their banned essays, fueling further discontent. Sympathizers in the liberal intelligentsia organized covert funds to support exiled artists, bridging the gap between radical activism and more moderate professional circles. This synergy created a broader cultural opposition that the Okhrana struggled to contain.

Terrorism, Provocateurs, and the Okhrana's Dilemma

The Persistence of Revolutionary Violence

Despite the crushing measures, radical groups continued to plot acts of terror. The Socialist Revolutionaries (SRs) maintained a "Combat Organization," carrying out high-profile assassinations of government officials they deemed responsible for oppression. Bombings and shootings kept the population in a state of tension, and each new attack prompted calls from conservatives for even harsher policing. The regime escalated infiltration efforts, determined to preempt future acts before bombs could explode.

Yet, the Okhrana's successes were mixed. While they did occasionally thwart plots, they often discovered them only after infiltration by agent provocateurs. Such agents sometimes egged on unsuspecting radicals, coaxing them into more dangerous schemes that justified brutal crackdowns. Public knowledge of these provocations discredited the secret police, suggesting they were manufacturing conspiracies as much as they were preventing them. Indeed, some historians argue that these tactics radicalized individuals who might otherwise have remained moderate.

The Risk of Moral Confusion

For the Okhrana leadership, this approach posed ethical and operational dilemmas. Encouraging or facilitating acts of violence to entrap suspects risked losing moral authority in the eyes of the public and even among some officials. In certain cases, agent provocateurs gathered significant personal power, playing both sides for profit or personal vendettas. The lines between genuine revolutionary cells and state-manufactured conspiracies blurred.

Meanwhile, ordinary citizens, seeing news of bombings and arrests, often felt trapped between fear of terrorism and fear of the secret police. For many, the question became less about whether they supported the regime or the revolution, and more about simple survival. Trust eroded in official narratives, fueling the idea that the entire governance structure was corrupt and that genuine redress of grievances might only come through drastic change.

Exile Communities as Incubators of Revolution

Bolsheviks and Mensheviks in Siberia

The split within the Russian Social Democratic Labor Party (RSDLP) in 1903 into Bolsheviks and Mensheviks led to spirited debates that often continued in exile. Figures like Joseph Stalin, Lev Kamenev, and others spent years in Siberian banishment. Though conditions were harsh, these exiles used the time to hone ideological positions and cultivate networks. Letters and secret dispatches from exile reached party members in European Russia, shaping strategy and forging solidarity.

In some respects, Siberian exile proved ironically beneficial for the revolutionary cause. Freed from immediate police harassment—though still under local supervision—exiled party leaders had the opportunity to reflect on political tactics. They engaged in theoretical study of Marxism, wrote leaflets, and established communication lines with foreign-based exiles like Vladimir Lenin in Switzerland. By 1905, as domestic upheaval surged, many exiles found ways to escape or secure amnesties, returning home to fan the flames of rebellion armed with refined ideas.

Cultural and Educational Activities

Not all exiles were professional revolutionaries. Some were teachers, doctors, or journalists caught in the net of suspicion. In remote villages, they taught reading, basic hygiene, and crafts, inadvertently raising the cultural level of local peasant populations. These exiles introduced modern ideas about hygiene, crop rotation, or cooperative organization, sometimes improving living standards.

Such activities ran parallel to the exiles' political mission. While the Okhrana worried about indoctrination, local peasants often appreciated the practical help. Over time, a peculiar dynamic emerged: exiles whose presence was intended to hamper revolutionary activity instead earned respect from local communities, creating pockets of sympathy for the broader cause of reform or revolution. Upon returning to European Russia, these individuals carried with them firsthand knowledge of the empire's vastness and inequalities.

Shifts in Strategy and the 1905 Revolution's Aftermath

The October Manifesto and Partial Liberalization

The year 1905 saw Russia explode in widespread revolt, culminating in strikes, armed uprisings, and the establishment of workers' councils (soviets) in some cities. Facing chaos, Nicholas II conceded, issuing the October Manifesto which promised a constitution and an elected Duma. The regime hoped this move would split the opposition, placating liberals while isolating hardcore revolutionaries. For a brief period, censorship eased, and political parties publicly formed, giving a semblance of openness.

Yet, the Okhrana remained active. Even as newspapers published more freely, secret agents kept close tabs on newly legalized parties—like the Constitutional Democrats (Kadets) and the more radical socialists. When the immediate revolutionary crisis passed, the government reasserted control, arresting or exiling those who violated the vague limits of permissible dissent. Many revolutionaries saw the October Manifesto as a strategic retreat by the tsar, not a genuine transformation of autocracy.

Stolypin's Reforms and Renewed Repression

In the post-1905 period, Prime Minister Pyotr Stolypin attempted a two-pronged approach: land reforms to create a conservative class of prosperous peasants, and harsh crackdowns on revolutionary violence. Under his watch, the Okhrana utilized "field courts-martial" and speedy trials to execute suspected terrorists. Exile continued en masse. But even these measures did not eradicate the underground networks entirely.

While some peasants benefited from Stolypin's policies, much of the countryside remained dissatisfied, and the memory of 1905's bloodshed lingered. Exiles returned or escaped, bringing fresh impetus to clandestine organizations. The Okhrana, for all its resources, struggled to snuff out the resilience that years of oppression had seeded.

CHAPTER 18

THE SPREAD OF REVOLUTIONARY TERROR AND GOVERNMENT RETALIATION

Introduction

By the mid-1900s, Russia had become a cauldron of smoldering discontent. The humiliating end of the Russo-Japanese War, the massacre of peaceful demonstrators on Bloody Sunday, and the wave of strikes and uprisings in 1905 all eroded whatever lingering trust the populace had in Tsar Nicholas II's regime. Although the October Manifesto promised a new era of constitutional government, real power remained concentrated in the hands of the autocracy and its allies. The partially elected Duma offered a narrow avenue for political expression, but key levers of authority—military command, police forces, and ultimate lawmaking—stayed firmly under imperial control.

In this fraught atmosphere, radical groups on both sides intensified their strategies. Revolutionary organizations, frustrated with limited reforms, resorted to bombings, assassinations, and expropriations (robberies for funding) to undermine the state and finance their cause. The most active among them were the Socialist Revolutionaries (SRs) and certain factions within the Socialist Democratic movements (Bolsheviks or aligned splinters), though anarchist cells and other smaller groups also participated. The government, for its part, cracked down harder, arming the police with broader powers of arrest and employing the army to suppress strikes. The secret police (Okhrana) and local authorities used raids, show trials, and executions in an attempt to extinguish revolutionary fervor.

This chapter explores the interplay between escalating revolutionary terror and the regime's equally forceful retaliation from about 1906 to 1909. We will see how acts of violence—both by radicals and by the state—shaped public perceptions, drove political debate, and contributed to a climate of fear and suspicion. We will also examine how everyday people were caught in this crossfire, increasingly convinced that peaceful change might be impossible. These years of bloodshed and revenge set the stage for deeper polarization within Russian society, foreshadowing the seismic upheavals still to come.

Radical Tactics: Bombs, Assassinations, and Expropriations

The Socialist Revolutionary Combat Organization

Of all the radical groups operating in the aftermath of 1905, the Socialist Revolutionaries (SRs) stood out for their emphasis on direct, often violent action. While the main SR party platform championed land reform and peasant-based socialism, its clandestine "Combat Organization" specialized in terror. Composed of dedicated operatives trained in explosives and covert operations, it targeted high-profile government officials—governors, police chiefs, ministers—seen as enforcers of autocratic repression.

The logic behind such assassinations was straightforward: eliminate oppressive figures and demoralize the ruling apparatus. However, these attacks often caused collateral damage. A bomb intended for a single official might detonate prematurely, killing or maiming bystanders. Nonetheless, the Combat Organization found support among radicals who viewed violence as the only language the Tsarist state would heed. Each successful assassination was celebrated in underground newspapers, fueling a cycle of admiration and recruitment among younger, disillusioned activists.

Expropriation for Funding

Revolutionary activity required money—for printing presses, safe houses, and living expenses for underground operatives. Groups like the Bolsheviks and certain SR factions turned to expropriations, effectively armed robberies of banks, mail trains, or wealthy institutions. Some cells rationalized these robberies as "confiscations" of the aristocracy's ill-gotten wealth.

Among the most notorious expropriations was the 1907 Tiflis bank heist, reportedly orchestrated by high-ranking Bolsheviks including Joseph Stalin. During that operation, grenades and gunfire claimed lives in a crowded city square, shocking local residents. While the funds were funneled into revolutionary coffers, the violence outraged many—raising moral questions even within the radical movements themselves. Some members argued that terrorizing ordinary citizens for money undermined the revolution's moral authority. Yet the lure of significant funds and the perceived urgency of the struggle often overrode such concerns.

Splits and Debates Within Revolutionary Circles

Not all revolutionaries agreed on the extent or utility of terror. The SR party faced internal disputes between those committed to peaceful political participation (through the Duma or local councils) and those insisting on armed struggle. Marxist groups, too, were divided. Many Mensheviks favored a more incremental approach, working through labor unions and the nascent Duma to improve conditions. Bolsheviks, led by Vladimir Lenin, sometimes employed militant tactics, though even within their ranks opinions varied about expropriations and assassinations.

As terror escalated, these divisions deepened. Some activists questioned whether random bombings alienated the very masses whose support the revolutionaries needed. Others countered that no meaningful change could occur without striking fear into the heart of the regime. The state's relentless crackdowns only added fuel to the argument that peaceful methods were futile. By 1907, a kind of militant fatalism took hold among many cells, as each new wave of arrests or executions spurred them to respond with more violence.

The State Strikes Back: Stolypin and "Field Courts-Martial"

Pyotr Stolypin's Dual Strategy

After the 1905 Revolution, Nicholas II appointed Pyotr Stolypin as Minister of Internal Affairs and later Prime Minister. Stolypin believed Russia could be stabilized through a combination of stern repression and selective modernization. On one hand, he initiated land reforms aimed at creating a class of prosperous, conservative peasants who would uphold the empire's traditional order. On the other, he championed ruthless action against terrorists and revolutionaries—hoping to root out subversion before it could spread again.

Stolypin introduced a system of "field courts-martial" in mid-1906, allowing for rapid trials of suspected terrorists. These courts required little evidence, operated outside the usual judicial processes, and could impose sentences—often hanging—within days. The gallows earned the grim nickname "Stolypin's necktie." Critics charged that these courts bypassed basic legal rights, leading to numerous miscarriages of justice. Nonetheless, the prime minister insisted that only swift, severe punishment would deter further attacks.

Crackdown on Political Freedoms

Alongside these emergency courts, Stolypin curtailed freedoms grudgingly granted after 1905. Newspapers once again faced tight censorship if they criticized the monarchy or published details about trials. Police gained the power to exile suspects administratively—no trial necessary—if they were deemed likely troublemakers. Meetings of political parties were restricted; the Duma's more outspoken deputies risked harassment or arrest if they ventured too far in denouncing government policies.

In effect, the "reaction" that followed 1905 sought to roll back much of the October Manifesto's spirit. While the Duma continued to convene, it was carefully managed; the electoral system was reformed to favor landowners and wealthy urbanites, minimizing representation for workers and peasants. This partial liberalization satisfied some moderates but left radicals furious. Underground presses denounced Stolypin as an "executioner" and warned that his methods only confirmed the regime's inability to enact genuine reforms.

The Okhrana's Heightened Role

To enforce this renewed crackdown, the Okhrana expanded its infiltration of radical networks. Agents provocateurs entrenched themselves in major cities, orchestrating or at least facilitating terror plots that would then be "uncovered" to justify further arrests. Some believed that the Okhrana tried to push revolutionaries into violence, ensuring a steady stream of public "victories" against conspiracies. The risk, of course, was that these manipulations also caused real harm, as bombs detonated or shootouts erupted in public spaces.

Ordinary citizens found themselves living under increased scrutiny. Police demanded internal passports at every turn, patrolled worker districts more aggressively, and used "domiciliary visits" to rummage through homes at will. If any pamphlets or suspicious letters were found, entire families could face exile or prison. Fear permeated daily life; informers could be anywhere—coworkers, neighbors, even extended relatives. For many Russians, the dreams of 1905's revolution, with its hope for broad freedoms, turned into nightmares of state surveillance and arbitrary violence.

The Spiral of Violence: High-Profile Assassinations

The Murder of Key Officials

Despite Stolypin's harsh measures, radicals continued to strike. Some of the boldest attacks targeted influential administrators known for brutal crackdowns. In August 1906, General Fyodor Dubasov, Governor-General of Moscow, narrowly escaped a bombing. Numerous local police chiefs were less fortunate, killed by SR combat cells who declared their acts vengeance for peasants flogged or workers shot in prior protests.

Stolypin himself became a prime target. In August 1906, terrorists bombed his residence in St. Petersburg, killing several guards and members of his household. Though Stolypin and his family survived, the incident underscored the vulnerability of even the highest officials. The prime minister responded with intensified repressive methods, convinced that only unwavering severity would curb the wave of terror. Each side believed the other's brutality justified further escalation.

Public Reaction to Terrorist Acts

Revolutionary violence elicited mixed feelings among ordinary Russians. Some workers and peasants hailed assassinations of notoriously cruel officials, seeing them as acts of justice in a lawless empire. Others condemned the bloodshed, lamenting that bombs and bullets often harmed bystanders and alienated potential supporters of reform. The mass of the rural population remained largely uninvolved in direct action, focused on daily survival.

In the cities, a portion of the middle class, once sympathetic to moderate reform, recoiled from the chaos. They viewed assassinations as proof that radicals endangered public safety, potentially derailing economic progress. Newspapers alternated between outraged headlines about "murderous fanatics" and quietly acknowledging the social grievances that fueled such extremism. The monarchy exploited these sentiments, portraying itself as a bulwark against anarchy. Yet the very presence of so many outraged voices underscored a deeper national schism that mere condemnations could not resolve.

The Government's Heavy Hand: Mass Executions and Repressions

Executions and "Stolypin's Neckties"

Field courts-martial reached their peak of activity between 1906 and 1909. Estimates vary, but hundreds—perhaps thousands—of suspects were executed during these years, often within days of arrest. Hangings replaced the more public spectacle of firing squads or beheadings; it was deemed a faster, less disruptive method. However, rumors of gallows set up in local squares persisted, sowing terror among entire communities.

This wave of state violence served multiple aims: it decimated terrorist cells, intimidated prospective revolutionaries, and signaled to conservative elites that the government was in control. Yet it also created martyrs. Young men and women went to the scaffold proclaiming their loyalty to "the people," urging the crowd to continue the fight. Underground newspapers lionized these figures, publishing farewell letters and final speeches that reached far-flung reading circles, reinforcing the romantic image of self-sacrifice.

Punitive Expeditions in the Countryside

Beyond the cities, the regime dispatched punitive expeditions to quell peasant unrest. These expeditions, comprising troops and loyal Cossack units, swept through districts where uprisings had flared. Alleged ringleaders were summarily tried—or not tried at all—before being flogged or executed. Entire villages might be fined or forced to supply grain to feed the army. Houses were burned as a warning against future revolts.

Such tactics deepened rural antagonism toward the central government. While some peasants grudgingly submitted, others took to the forests, forming outlaw bands that raided estate owners and sabotaged roads or telegraph lines. Religious sects, national minorities, and older populist networks sometimes provided cover or resources to these fugitives, fostering an underground economy of defiance. The net effect was a sense that large swaths of the empire existed in a state of low-grade civil war, with the official state and armed peasants locked in cycles of violence and reprisal.

The Duma's Limited Role and Mounting Frustrations

Elections and Political Maneuvering

Following the October Manifesto, Russia experienced a series of Duma elections between 1906 and 1907. The first two Dumas were relatively radical, featuring sizable blocs of liberals (Cadets) and left-leaning deputies. They clashed repeatedly with Stolypin and the tsar over issues like land redistribution, amnesty for political prisoners, and civil rights. In response, Nicholas II dissolved the Duma twice, each time rewriting the electoral laws to favor conservative landowners and wealthy city dwellers.

By the time of the Third Duma (1907–1912), the body was more docile, dominated by Octobrists (moderates) and Rightists (monarchists). Though some reforms were debated—like improvements in education or local self-government—major structural changes were off the table. Revolutionaries denounced the Duma as a sham, a fig leaf covering the autocracy's iron fist. Even moderate deputies realized their power was severely constrained, resenting the unrelenting influence of the tsar's ministers and the security apparatus.

Public Disillusionment and Apathy

As terror and repression intensified, many ordinary Russians found themselves in a fog of confusion. Hopes for meaningful parliamentary reform receded when each Duma proved incapable of halting violence or alleviating grinding poverty.

Labor strikes continued but were met with arrests; peasants grumbled about the slow pace of Stolypin's land reforms. Middle-class professionals, initially energized by the idea of a constitutional monarchy, saw proposals stalled or watered down in committees overshadowed by bureaucrats.

This disillusionment sometimes morphed into apathy. Exhausted by turmoil, people stopped looking to politics for solutions. Family survival, staying out of trouble, and avoiding police scrutiny became paramount. Yet beneath the surface, radical elements continued forging networks. Fear gave them a recruiting tool: "The state is waging war on us," they argued, "so we have no choice but to strike back." Even among the disillusioned, seeds of future revolt lay dormant, waiting for the right catalyst.

The Legacy of Violence and Repression

The Long Shadow of Retaliation

By 1909, the number of political executions and assassinations had gradually declined. Many radical leaders had been killed, imprisoned, or forced into foreign exile. Some cells ceased operations due to lack of funds or infiltration by provocateurs. The state, though battered by international embarrassment and internal upheaval, maintained a grip on power. In official circles, this was considered a victory—a demonstration that unwavering toughness could pacify dissent.

Yet the empire remained haunted by memories of these brutal years. Families who lost loved ones to the gallows or to random bomb attacks carried deep resentments. The monarchy's moral standing was severely compromised; even conservative supporters whispered about the cruelty of field courts-martial. Intellectuals, once ambivalent, gradually shifted toward a more decisive anti-regime stance, convinced that peaceful evolution was a fantasy under an autocracy that repeatedly resorted to violence.

Radicalization and Strategic Shifts

For the revolutionary movement, the period of intense terror and retaliation led to shifts in strategy. The SR party, disillusioned with constant bloodshed and infiltration, scaled back its Combat Organization. Some members gravitated to broad-based peasant organizing, seeking to harness rural frustration more systematically. Others joined socialist parties like the Bolsheviks or Mensheviks, preferring to focus on labor strikes and political education rather than sporadic violence.

Bolsheviks also underwent a transformation. While still open to militant tactics, they began emphasizing the consolidation of worker-based organizations (soviets), trade unions, and clandestine party structures that could mobilize large numbers when the next revolutionary moment arrived. They understood that assassinations alone wouldn't topple the autocracy; only a mass movement, possibly with the army's involvement, could succeed.

Though quiescent on the surface by 1909, the empire's tensions lay thick as winter ice on a Russian river. Beneath that frozen crust, currents of anger and hope still flowed. The harsh retaliations from 1906 to 1909 taught revolutionaries about the dangers of open conflict but also hardened their resolve to build a more disciplined and wide-reaching movement. Meanwhile, state loyalists believed they had subdued the revolutionary tide—but that belief would be tested again.

CHAPTER 19

THE FINAL DAYS OF THE ROMANOV DYNASTY

Introduction

By the early 1910s, the Romanov dynasty had reigned over Russia for more than three centuries. Yet beneath the pomp of court ceremonies and the glitter of imperial palaces, the empire was in disarray. Discontent simmered among industrial workers subjected to grueling conditions, peasants chafed under archaic land laws, and minority nationalities despised Russification policies. The monarchy, led by Tsar Nicholas II, had survived the revolutionary tremors of 1905 through a mix of partial reforms and brutal crackdowns. But the seeds of deeper upheaval remained, nurtured by unresolved grievances, growing political consciousness, and the memory of repeated betrayals by the state.

This chapter traces the final decade of the Romanov dynasty—roughly 1910 to 1917—focusing on the events and personalities that propelled Russia toward a catastrophic endgame. We will see how World War I ignited national fervor but quickly revealed dire weaknesses in Russia's military and infrastructure. We will examine the scandalous influence of the mysterious peasant-healer, Grigory Rasputin, on the royal family, which discredited the monarchy in the eyes of nobles and commoners alike. As the war dragged on with devastating casualties, food shortages, and political chaos, Nicholas II's hold on power slipped away. The monarchy's collapse in the February Revolution of 1917, followed by the tragic fate of the royal family, would bring the Romanov line to a violent close—ending centuries of imperial rule and opening a chapter of even greater turmoil.

Mounting Tensions and the Shadow of Rasputin

A Court Besieged by Intrigue

Even after the bloodshed and repression of the post-1905 years, the Romanov court tried to present an image of stability. Tsar Nicholas II and Empress Alexandra hosted lavish balls at the Winter Palace, and foreign dignitaries marveled at the empire's extravagant traditions. Behind this façade, however, the royal couple grew increasingly isolated. Nicholas, a gentle but indecisive autocrat, shied away from robust policy debates. Alexandra, deeply religious and suspicious of the court elite, formed a tight circle around herself—primarily ladies-in-waiting who shared her mystical devotions and unwavering belief in the Tsar's divine mandate.

These circumstances allowed rumors, plots, and rivalries to fester. Members of the extended Romanov family, as well as high-ranking nobles and ministers, jockeyed for influence. Many recognized that Nicholas was a poor strategist, prone to placing personal loyalty above competence when appointing officials. To secure favor, courtiers showered Alexandra with gifts and flattery, hoping she would whisper their names in the Tsar's ear. The Okhrana, still vigilant, spied not only on revolutionaries but also on aristocrats suspected of disloyalty. Paranoia gripped the corridors of power, weakening the monarchy from within.

The Rise of Rasputin

Amid this environment stepped Grigory Rasputin, a Siberian peasant who presented himself as a starets—a wandering holy man with mystical healing powers. Rasputin's greatest inroad to the royal family came through the Tsarevich Alexei, heir to the throne. Alexei suffered from hemophilia, a painful and dangerous blood disorder. When doctors failed to cure him, Rasputin's prayers and confident presence seemed to bring temporary relief. Alexandra became convinced that Rasputin was divinely sent to safeguard her son's life.

By 1910–1912, Rasputin's influence had grown significantly. He gained unprecedented access to the royal court, offering counsel on spiritual and political matters. Stories abounded of his coarse manners, rumored sexual liaisons, and questionable drinking habits. Yet Alexandra staunchly defended him, insisting that critics were jealous or blinded by malice. Nicholas, reluctant to upset his wife and frightened of Alexei's health crises, tolerated Rasputin's presence despite misgivings. Ministers who questioned Rasputin's power found themselves sidelined or fired.

The Gathering Storm of World War I

Russia's Entry into the Conflict

While the court wrestled with internal intrigue, Europe moved closer to catastrophe. The complex system of alliances, fueled by imperial rivalries and a climate of militarism, sparked a chain reaction after the assassination of Archduke Franz Ferdinand in June 1914. Russia, allied with Serbia, mobilized its massive army when Austria-Hungary declared war on the Serbs. Germany, allied with Austria-Hungary, in turn declared war on Russia. Within weeks, the Great Powers plunged into World War I.

In the initial surge of patriotic fervor, Russians of all classes rallied behind the Tsar. Citizens thronged city squares, chanting slogans of loyalty to the empire. Factories churned out munitions, and young men volunteered for the front. Many believed the war would unify the nation, putting an end to internal strife. Indeed, early skirmishes in East Prussia and Galicia saw Russian troops advancing. But these successes were short-lived. A lack of modern weaponry, poor logistical planning, and the vastness of the front soon exacted a terrible toll.

Catastrophic Losses and Logistical Failures

By 1915, the Russian army had suffered staggering defeats. Germany's well-trained forces, equipped with machine guns and heavy artillery, inflicted massive casualties on the poorly supplied Russian infantry. Soldiers complained of insufficient rifles, shells, and medical supplies. Some units lacked boots, forced to march barefoot in freezing conditions. Railroad bottlenecks delayed reinforcements and rations. Correspondence from the front revealed disorganized leadership, with generals contradicting each other's orders.

As the body count soared, public morale plummeted. Wounded soldiers returned in droves, recounting horror stories of trench warfare, hunger, and incompetent officers. In cities, the cost of basic goods escalated; bread lines stretched for blocks as grain shipments were diverted or delayed. Factories, pressed to produce war materials, saw labor unrest intensify. The government's attempts to quell strikes with police raids only fueled discontent. Meanwhile, war expenditures ballooned, forcing the state to print more money—spurring inflation that wiped out modest wages. The illusions of a swift, glorious campaign lay in tatters, replaced by despair and anger.

Rasputin's Influence and the Discrediting of the Court

Ministerial Chaos and Alexandra's Role

As Nicholas spent more time at military headquarters (the Stavka) directing war strategy—or attempting to—he left much of the day-to-day governance in

Alexandra's hands. The Empress, distrusting many noble families who scorned Rasputin, replaced ministers on a whim, guided by the starets' counsel. Over a short span, key posts—Interior, War, Foreign Affairs—changed hands repeatedly. Decisions about ammunition production, transportation, and economic regulation often went to men with little experience, chosen primarily for their loyalty to the Empress and Rasputin.

This revolving-door approach to governance alarmed the Duma and moderate conservatives alike, who saw no coherent war strategy. Secret police reports indicated a severe drop in public confidence. High society gossiped about Rasputin's rumored affairs with ladies of the court, painting him as a sinister puppet master behind Alexandra. Caricatures depicted the Tsarina kneeling at Rasputin's feet, or Rasputin presiding over the royal family's dinner table, reinforcing the image of a monarchy under occult manipulation.

The Rasputin Scandals

Stories of Rasputin's debauchery circulated widely in both underground pamphlets and foreign newspapers. Some claimed he belonged to a heretical sect that practiced bizarre rituals, though historians debate the veracity of these accusations. Eyewitnesses recounted seeing Rasputin stumble drunkenly through the streets, bragging of his sway over the royal family. The British ambassador described him as a "dangerous charlatan." Even moderate monarchists implored Nicholas to exile Rasputin, arguing that his mere presence tarnished the Romanovs' reputation.

But the Tsar refused, convinced by Alexandra's desperate pleas that removing Rasputin would endanger Alexei's life. With each new scandal, calls for Rasputin's removal grew louder, culminating in clandestine plots among aristocrats to eliminate him physically. Meanwhile, the empire's war effort faltered, fueling talk that the monarchy was hopelessly compromised by an unholy trinity: an inept Tsar, a meddling Empress, and a depraved "holy man."

Intensifying Crisis on the Home Front

Economic Breakdown and Food Shortages

By late 1916, Russia's economy teetered under the pressures of total war. Millions of peasants had been conscripted, reducing agricultural output. Rail transport prioritized military shipments, causing grain to rot in station warehouses while bread prices in cities skyrocketed. Inflation galloped forward; wages could not keep pace. Factory owners jacked up production quotas but struggled to procure raw materials, leading to sporadic layoffs that further fueled worker anger.

Strikes became more frequent and more organized. Protests for bread or higher wages escalated into political demands, with workers calling for an end to the war and the abdication of Nicholas II. Some labor organizers, aligned with socialist factions, used the turmoil to spread radical ideas. Meanwhile, in rural areas, rumors spread that "the Tsar wants to give us land, but wicked nobles and officials block his will," echoing older peasant myths. People felt betrayed by local authorities, many of whom profiteered from grain sales on the black market.

Duma Outcry and Calls for Reform

Even the conservative-leaning Duma grew outspoken. Leading figures like Pavel Milyukov delivered fiery speeches denouncing ministerial corruption and the Tsar's blind faith in Rasputin. Milyukov famously asked, "Is this stupidity or treason?" referencing the leadership's dismal handling of the war. Though the Duma lacked direct power to dismiss ministers, its public debates reverberated. Newspapers published sensational accounts of mismanagement, further eroding the monarchy's credibility.

Nicholas responded by proroguing the Duma or ignoring its resolutions, reinforcing the impression that he was out of touch. Some Duma deputies privately discussed forming a "provisional government" if the crisis worsened. This talk of usurping the Tsar's prerogatives—once unthinkable in conservative circles—signaled how desperate the situation had become. Many realized that if Nicholas did not act decisively to reform, the alternative might be a revolutionary explosion.

The Assassination of Rasputin

A Desperate Conspiracy

By late 1916, a group of aristocrats, led by Prince Felix Yusupov and Grand Duke Dmitri Pavlovich, decided Rasputin had to die for the monarchy's survival. They feared that unless Rasputin's influence was severed, military collapse and popular revolt would destroy the Romanovs. In December 1916, these conspirators invited Rasputin to Yusupov's palace under the pretext of meeting high-society ladies.

Accounts vary on the exact sequence of events, but the conspirators laced cakes and wine with poison, which appeared to have little effect on Rasputin. Panicking, they resorted to shooting him multiple times. Legend holds that Rasputin still clung to life, crawling away before being shot again and possibly beaten. They dumped his body into the icy Neva River. When discovered days later, he was definitively dead—though rumors claimed he had survived the initial attempts.

Aftermath and the Dynastic Unraveling

The conspirators hoped Rasputin's death would reinvigorate public faith in the monarchy, but their plot backfired. Alexandra was distraught, convinced her son's health and the empire itself were now doomed. Nicholas, returning from the front, expressed fury at the lawlessness of aristocrats taking matters into their own hands. Neither the Tsar nor the Empress recognized that Rasputin's murder reflected the final collapse of loyal court unity.

Commoners, for their part, were unmoved by Rasputin's death; it did nothing to solve food shortages or end the war. Instead, it underscored that the monarchy was in chaos, with powerful nobles bypassing imperial authority to commit murder. The press had a field day, printing lurid details of the crime scene, rehashing tales of Rasputin's debauchery. Far from restoring faith, the assassination highlighted the monarchy's inability to govern effectively. Within weeks, the empire would plunge into revolution, making Rasputin's murder a grim footnote in the Romanov saga.

The February Revolution of 1917

Mass Protests in Petrograd

In early 1917, protests over bread shortages erupted in Petrograd (the new name for St. Petersburg, changed in 1914 to sound less German). Women leading the queues for bread began chanting anti-war and anti-government slogans. Factories joined in, sparking a general strike. Soldiers in garrisons around the city, many of them raw conscripts tired of war and loyal to no one but themselves, sympathized with protesters. When ordered to fire on crowds, some regiments mutinied, refusing to shoot fellow Russians.

Over a matter of days, Petrograd spun out of Nicholas II's control. Police vanished from the streets or were overwhelmed. Workers and soldiers formed the Petrograd Soviet, an assembly to coordinate demands and manage local order. Meanwhile, the Duma took the extraordinary step of forming a Provisional Committee to restore stability—without explicit imperial sanction. By the last week of February (early March in the Western calendar), calls for the Tsar's abdication echoed across the capital.

Nicholas II's Abdication

Isolated at the military headquarters in Mogilev, Nicholas initially dismissed reports of unrest as exaggerated. But telegrams from ministers and generals became frantic, urging him to concede constitutional reforms or risk losing the throne. Belatedly, the Tsar boarded a train for Petrograd, hoping to negotiate. However, railway workers diverted his train, preventing him from reaching the capital. Upon realizing the gravity of the revolt, Nicholas's generals—fearing total military collapse—insisted he abdicate to preserve order.

On March 2, 1917 (Old Style), Nicholas II renounced his throne for himself and for his son Alexei. He briefly tried to pass the crown to his brother, Grand Duke Michael, who refused the burden without a vote of confidence from a future constituent assembly. The Romanov dynasty's rule ended abruptly. Shock spread through Europe. In Petrograd, a jubilant crowd tore down imperial emblems. Soldiers replaced insignias with red ribbons, and the new Provisional Government declared the start of a new era.

Captivity and Execution of the Imperial Family

Arrest and Temporary Exile

Following abdication, Nicholas II and his family were placed under house arrest in the Alexander Palace at Tsarskoye Selo. While the Provisional Government debated their fate, the royal family lived in relative comfort compared to typical prisoners. Still, they were under guard, their movements restricted, and Alexandra's heartbreak at the turn of events mingled with concern for Alexei's health.

As the Provisional Government struggled to keep control amid rising Bolshevik influence, the question of what to do with the Romanovs became urgent. Fearing that monarchists might rally around Nicholas to stage a counter-revolution, officials decided to move the family to Tobolsk in Siberia in August 1917. There, conditions were modest but not brutal: they resided in a governor's house, had a small retinue, and the children continued lessons. Yet the pall of uncertainty hung over them—would they be put on trial, sent abroad, or quietly disposed of?

The Bolsheviks' Seizure of Power

In October 1917, the Bolsheviks, led by Lenin, overthrew the Provisional Government. Civil war soon engulfed Russia, with the Red (Bolshevik) forces battling an array of White (anti-Bolshevik) armies. The Romanovs were now in the hands of a regime that viewed them as symbols of centuries-long oppression. By spring 1918, with civil war intensifying, the Bolsheviks transferred the family again—first to Ekaterinburg, a stronghold of Soviet power in the Urals.

Under harsher confinement, the family's privileges disappeared. Guards monitored every move, restricting their letters, limiting rations, and dismantling any illusions of future restoration. Meanwhile, White armies advanced, hoping to rescue the royal hostages. As these forces drew nearer to Ekaterinburg, local Bolshevik authorities, fearing the Romanovs might be liberated and used as a rallying point, received a fateful directive.

Execution in Ekaterinburg

On the night of July 16–17, 1918, the family—Nicholas, Alexandra, their five children, and four loyal attendants—were awakened and led to a basement room under the pretext of safety. There, a squad of Bolshevik secret police (Cheka) informed them that the local Soviet had decided on immediate execution. Gunfire erupted. The Tsar and Empress died quickly, but the children, protected by diamonds sewn into their clothing, required multiple shots or bayonet thrusts. The bodies were hastily removed, doused with acid, and hidden in a forest grave, details kept secret for decades.

News of the execution shocked the world. Though many Russians reviled the monarchy, the killing of children especially evoked horror. The Bolsheviks defended it as a necessary act to prevent monarchist forces from exploiting the family. For others, it marked a chilling new phase of revolutionary violence—one that recognized no sanctity in the old regime's bloodline. With this final act, the Romanov dynasty ended in brutality that echoed the terror of the preceding years.

Conclusion

The last days of the Romanov dynasty stand as a grim testament to how an ancient monarchy, weakened by incompetence, war, scandal, and internal division, could collapse with startling speed. Nicholas II's mismanagement of World War I and tolerance for Rasputin's meddling alienated nearly every social stratum, from aristocrats to workers. Economic meltdown, food shortages, and the brazen disorder of the imperial court unraveled the empire's already tattered unity. When the February Revolution erupted, the Tsar found almost no loyal defenders, forced to abdicate in a railway car far from his capital.

The Provisional Government, too weak and fragmented to forge a new order, yielded power to the Bolsheviks that autumn. Their victory sealed the Romanovs' fate, culminating in a blood-soaked finale in a Ural basement. This violent end encapsulated the turmoil that had been building for decades, revealing the depth of anger and disillusionment among Russia's diverse peoples. From Rasputin's sinister hold on the royal court to the chaos of war and revolution, the final days of the Romanov dynasty remain one of history's stark reminders that even the grandest autocracies can dissolve into chaos when faith in leadership vanishes.

In our next and final chapter, we will reflect on the broader legacy of fear and oppression left by centuries of shifting rule—underscoring how the cycles of violence, paranoia, and authoritarianism reverberated beyond the Romanov era, shaping the trajectory of modern Russia. The chaos that ended the imperial line opened the door to new forms of governance, but also new terrors that would define the 20th century in unimaginable ways.

CHAPTER 20

A LEGACY OF FEAR AND OPPRESSION

Introduction

From the earliest Slavic settlements in the vast forests of Eastern Europe to the violent end of the Romanov dynasty, Russia's history abounds with cycles of conquest, harsh rule, and relentless struggles for power. Wars, invasions, and internal strife repeatedly forced rulers to rely on intimidation and brute force to maintain authority. Over the centuries, different regimes employed draconian tactics to prevent uprisings and stifle dissent. Fear became a governing tool as much as a reaction to foreign threats or domestic revolts.

In this final chapter, we reflect on how these patterns of fear and oppression evolved and persisted through eras of Kievan Rus, Mongol domination, the rise of Muscovy, the reign of autocratic tsars, and the eventual collapse of the Romanov dynasty. We will see how the cycles of mistrust, violence, and brutal crackdowns shaped Russian society, leaving a complex legacy that endured well beyond the monarchy's fall. This concluding look ties together recurring themes: the pervasive role of secret police and forced labor, the stifling of intellectual freedoms, the fragility of reform efforts under autocracy, and the price paid by millions of ordinary people caught under a system that prized centralized power above all else.

As we step back to take in the broader sweep of centuries, the question arises: Was Russia inevitably bound to follow a path of heavy-handed rule, or could alternatives have flourished had circumstances been different? While there is no simple answer, understanding how fear served as both a method and a consequence of governance may shed light on the complex roots of Russian political culture—one in which authority and terror were often intimately linked, even as aspirations for liberty emerged time and again.

Centuries of Turbulence and the Seeds of Fear

The Early Slavic World and Constant Threats

Fear as a political force can be traced back to the region's earliest days. During the era of Kievan Rus (9th–13th centuries), Slavic tribes navigated a dangerous landscape of raiding nomads, Viking influences, and shifting alliances. City-states like Kiev, Novgorod, and Vladimir were vulnerable to invasions by steppe nomads or rival princes. Leaders who managed to unite territories often resorted to punishing rebellions severely, mindful that unity was fragile. Even the great city of Kiev was not immune to conquest and pillage, culminating in the devastating Mongol invasion of the 13th century.

Under the Mongol Yoke (13th–15th centuries), fear reached a new level. The Golden Horde's demands for tribute, coupled with their brutal reprisals against defiance, enforced compliance. Local princes became enforcers for the Mongols, collecting taxes from their own people—often ruthlessly. Cities that resisted faced total destruction. The memory of these raids and the subjugation that followed left a deep imprint on the Russian psyche, embedding the idea that only strong centralized power could protect the land. This conviction carried forward as Muscovy rose to prominence, determined never again to be so vulnerable.

Establishing Muscovy's Supremacy

When Moscow emerged from under Mongol rule, rulers like Ivan III and Ivan IV (the Terrible) molded the region into a centralized state. Ivan the Terrible's Oprichnina—where a special police force terrorized boyars and commoners—became emblematic of how fear could be used internally to crush opposition. City after city witnessed public punishments or executions for anyone suspected of disloyalty. This model laid the groundwork for subsequent regimes to harness secret police forces, forced labor, and exile as standard political tools.

Although Russia occasionally experienced more moderate rulers—like some of the Romanovs who attempted cautious reforms—none fully dismantled the structures of fear-based governance. Peter the Great's modernization campaign advanced Russia's global stature but also underscored the idea that the state had the right to demand near-total obedience from its subjects. Catherine the Great continued to refine autocratic rule while intensifying control over serfs. In each case, the monarchy expanded territory and shaped new policies, but the reliance on strict power hierarchies and intimidation endured.

Tools of Oppression: Secret Police, Serfdom, and Exile

Surveillance and the Evolving Police Apparatus

Throughout Russian history, rulers developed specialized institutions to monitor and silence dissent. In medieval times, this took the form of local enforcers and roving detachments loyal to the tsar, but it culminated in more systematic agencies like the Third Section (under Nicholas I) and later the Department of State Police, commonly referred to as the Okhrana. These bureaus infiltrated society at every level. Clerks in government offices, priests, peasants, and even aristocrats could become informers, drawn by fear or promises of reward.

The methods ranged from hidden spying and mail interception to arbitrary arrest. Trials often included confessions obtained under duress, and sentences were swift and unforgiving—ranging from forced labor to exile in remote Siberian settlements. Over time, the machinery of surveillance perfected infiltration, employing agent provocateurs who incited revolutionaries to commit violent acts, thus providing a rationale for sweeping crackdowns.

The Burden of Serfdom

No examination of fear and oppression in Russia is complete without acknowledging serfdom—the binding of millions of peasants to landed estates. Dating from the 17th century and solidified by later legal codes, serfdom placed peasants under the near-absolute power of landlords. Families could be bought, sold, or punished at the master's whim. Rebellions, such as Pugachev's Uprising, were met with ferocious retaliation. While Alexander II's 1861 Emancipation technically freed peasants, heavy redemption payments and communal restrictions perpetuated economic bondage, leaving many still vulnerable to famine, debt, and exploitation.

The fear inculcated by serfdom extended far beyond the farm. Landlords, sometimes with local officials' collusion, could enforce discipline through brutal means. Failure to meet obligations invited floggings or exile to Siberia. This dynamic stifled rural innovation and literacy, as peasants had little incentive or freedom to pursue education or invest in long-term improvements. Fear also shaped how peasants perceived authority: the "little father" myth of the tsar coexisted with the dread that local nobles and bureaucrats held day-to-day power over life and livelihood.

Exile as a Means of Isolation

From early Muscovite times through the late Romanov era, exile was a favored method of removing threats without the spectacle of public trials or executions. State officials, revolutionaries, critical intellectuals, and minority leaders often found themselves marched off to Siberian settlements. Stripped of status, separated from families or forced to bring them along, exiles lived under constant surveillance. Some endured harsh climates and meager resources, effectively silenced by distance and the daily struggle for survival.

Ironically, exile communities sometimes became hotbeds of revolutionary thought. Individuals from various backgrounds—moderate liberals, radical populists, Marxists, or nationalist activists—congregated, forming networks that would influence Russia's future upheavals. Yet the immediate goal of exile was to instill fear among those who remained free: challenge the state, and you, too, could vanish into the frozen hinterlands.

The Psychological Dimension: Internalizing Fear

The Weight of Generational Trauma

Generations of Russians grew up in a milieu where arbitrary rule and violent punishments were normalized. The memory of Mongol devastations lingered in folk songs, while tales of brutal crackdowns under Ivan the Terrible passed into cultural lore. Each new wave of repression—be it under Peter the Great's forced modernization, Catherine's stifling of serfs, or Nicholas I's expansions of the secret police—reinforced a sense that dissent brought dire consequences. Families passed down cautionary tales, and communities learned to keep their heads low.

Folk expressions and proverbs emerged to warn against criticizing officials. In villages, rumor alone could endanger an entire family if authorities suspected sedition. The unpredictability of punishment—whether it came from local landowners, roving police squads, or the tsar's direct wrath—further heightened anxieties. Over time, many accepted fear as an immutable fact of life, stifling open debate and even shaping art, literature, and religion to avoid direct confrontation with authority.

Coping Mechanisms and Resistance

Yet this ingrained fear also spurred various forms of resistance. Intellectuals used allegory and coded language to critique oppression, as seen in works by Pushkin, Gogol, and later writers who navigated censorship. In peasants' daily lives, small acts of defiance—like hidden gatherings or mocking local officials in private jokes—offered emotional relief. Secret religious sects formed, sometimes combining Orthodox rites with anti-authoritarian messages. The fact that each wave of heavy-handed rule eventually triggered revolts—like the Time of Troubles, the Decembrist Revolt, Pugachev's Uprising, or the 1905 Revolution—highlights that suppressed anger could never be completely extinguished.

Importantly, fear was not monolithic. Nobles felt threatened by the possibility of tsarist reprisals or palace coups; city dwellers dreaded economic ruin and police raids; peasants feared hunger, forced conscription, and landlord brutality. These diverse fears sometimes prevented the formation of a united front against autocracy, allowing rulers to manipulate one group's anxieties to control another. The complexity of these tensions created a backdrop of mutual suspicion, undermining solidarity until moments of acute crisis forced alliances across social boundaries.

Illusions of Reform and Fragile Freedoms

Attempts at Modernization

In multiple eras, visionary or pragmatic rulers initiated reforms that momentarily loosened oppression. Alexander II's Great Reforms in the mid-19th century stand out, with the emancipation of serfs, the creation of local self-government (zemstvos), and judicial changes that introduced open courts and jury trials. While these moves hinted at a more liberal future, they also underscored how tenuous freedoms could be under autocracy. Conservative backlash, the Tsar's own reservations, and bureaucratic inertia blunted many of these reforms.

Similarly, the October Manifesto of 1905, issued under Nicholas II, promised civil liberties and a Duma, fueling hopes for constitutional government. Yet these concessions were quickly undercut: electoral laws were rigged, radical deputies were intimidated or jailed, and the secret police stymied honest political organizing. Instead of blossoming into a robust parliamentary system, the Duma became a battleground where real power was still wielded by the Tsar and his ministers. Thus, fleeting glimpses of greater liberty often ended in tightened repression when the throne felt threatened.

The Role of Intellectuals and the Middle Class

In societies riddled with fear, educated elites sometimes function as catalysts for reform. In Russia, an emergent middle class of merchants, professionals, and zemstvo members pressed for more systematic changes. They championed improved education, legal protections, and local autonomy, seeing these as essential for the empire's modernization. Writers, scientists, and progressive nobles joined these calls, believing that Russia could join Western Europe's trajectory if it shed its oppressive structures.

However, each wave of intellectual ferment collided with the state's conservative reflex. Censors banned literature deemed subversive, while secret police infiltrated academic circles. Universities became hotbeds of unrest, repeatedly shut down or placed under surveillance. Though some individuals were co-opted by officialdom, the broader community of thinkers often found itself marginalized and harassed. This pattern persisted into the final Romanov decades, leaving a legacy of unfulfilled liberal aspirations.

The Romanov Collapse and Post-Monarchy Echoes

The Final Implosion

When Nicholas II abdicated in 1917, it was the result of cumulative pressures that had been building for centuries. The war, with its catastrophic casualties, merely ignited a long-smoldering tinder of grievances. By that point, fear had lost its effectiveness as a unifying force. The armed forces no longer obeyed orders to shoot demonstrators; the Duma felt compelled to act independently; peasants and workers believed revolution was their only hope for relief. In this vacuum, the autocracy, which had maintained control through intimidation, swiftly disintegrated.

The Romanov downfall was thus both abrupt and deeply rooted. It showcased the risk any authoritarian regime faces when it depends on repression without addressing underlying social needs. Once fear ceases to paralyze the majority, the entire apparatus can unravel with surprising speed. Yet the end of Romanov rule did not erase the patterns established over centuries—new forms of power soon emerged, grappling with the same vast land, diverse populations, and entrenched social issues.

Transition to New Forms of Authority

Although this book concludes with the fall of the Romanovs, we can briefly note the immediate aftermath. The Provisional Government, which attempted to maintain order while continuing the war, quickly collapsed under renewed revolutionary pressures. The Bolshevik seizure of power in October 1917 opened the door to a different political order—one that would, in its own way, carry forward certain echoes of authoritarian control and reliance on enforced obedience. While such developments lie beyond the scope of our narrative, they underline how the legacies of fear and centralized authority did not vanish overnight with the abdication of the last tsar.

The Cost to Ordinary People

Cycles of Hardship

From the earliest serfs bound to medieval estates to industrial workers laboring under Tsarist factory discipline, ordinary Russians paid an enormous price for living in a society where harsh rule was normalized. The continuity of forced labor systems—serfdom, labor conscription, and penal servitude—disrupted family structures, perpetuated poverty, and stifled communal progress. Peasants scraping by on meager allotments faced repeated famines, high taxes, and the threat of brutality from landlords or officials. Factory hands endured twelve-hour shifts, relentless fines, and an ever-present police presence.

Rebellions—whether led by peasants, workers, or minority groups—often yielded only momentary victories or partial concessions. Rulers, fearing the slightest hint of disloyalty, clamped down swiftly, leaving behind mass arrests, executions, and exiles. Each cycle taught new generations the precariousness of challenging authority. Thus, while Russia's territory grew and its rulers boasted of imperial grandeur, the daily existence of most subjects remained precarious, overshadowed by the fear of retribution for dissent.

Emotional and Cultural Fallout

This environment of pervasive oppression influenced the way Russians expressed themselves culturally. Folk songs and epic poems frequently recounted the tragedies of lost villages, persecuted heroes, or the cruelty of distant overlords. Writers in the 19th century, from Pushkin to Dostoevsky, wrestled with themes of guilt, punishment, moral complexity, and redemption. Censorship forced creativity into subtexts and hidden critiques. Even religious life absorbed these strains, with some sects embracing martyrdom as a path to salvation.

Such cultural artifacts preserved a collective memory of suffering. They also provided glimpses of hope—visions of a redeemed future or a compassionate ruler who would break the chains. Yet as each new tsar ascended, the cycle of promises and betrayals persisted. This cumulative despair and fleeting optimism shaped a national mood that historians have often labeled as "fatalistic," though many Russians found ways to adapt and persevere.

Reflections on the Legacy

Patterns and Possibilities

In examining this long history, a paradox emerges: Russia repeatedly produced brilliant cultural achievements, robust forms of local self-organization (from medieval veches to zemstvos), and bursts of revolutionary energy that defied subjugation. Yet these potential sources of pluralism and freedom were consistently overshadowed by centralized rule and fear-based methods of control. One might argue that Russia's geography—its vast expanses and the need for a strong hand to repel invasions—favored authoritarian governance. Another viewpoint emphasizes missed opportunities for genuine reforms that could have balanced state power with societal needs.

The end of the Romanov dynasty in 1917 dramatically underscored that fear alone could not hold a modernizing society together indefinitely. External defeats, internal strife, and the monarchy's stubborn refusal to share power paved the way for collapse. While the monarchy's final demise was swift, its system of oppression had shaped Russian institutions and mindsets for centuries, leaving long-lasting marks on political habits, social structures, and cultural expressions.

Lessons for Future Generations

The story of fear and oppression in Russian history resonates beyond its borders, reminding us how regimes that rely on intimidation can appear stable until a crisis unravels the illusions. It also highlights the human cost: families torn by exiles, brilliant minds silenced by censorship, entire populations consigned to drudgery under rigid hierarchies. And yet, amid the darkness, acts of courage and vision emerged—revolts, literary masterpieces, communal solidarity—showing that the impulse for freedom and dignity endures even in the harshest conditions.

The Romanov era's final implosion closed one chapter but did not resolve the fundamental question: How can such a vast empire, with diverse peoples and a complicated past, reconcile a strong central authority with genuine liberties? That tension remained after the monarchy's downfall, shaping the next phase of Russia's evolution (though that phase lies beyond the scope of our focus here).

Conclusion

From Kievan Rus's fragile beginnings to the final breath of the Romanov dynasty, Russia's journey was shaped by the interplay of fear and power. Successive rulers, confronted by vast territories, external threats, and internal discord, resorted to severe measures to enforce unity. Secret police, forced labor, rigid hierarchies, and exiles all became staples of governance. Though certain rulers experimented with partial reforms—hoping to modernize the empire without undermining their authority—none succeeded in creating a stable, open society free of oppression.

Over centuries, this approach carved deep ruts into the nation's psyche, influencing everything from social relations to creative expression. It also sowed seeds of rebellion, as oppressed communities refused to relinquish dreams of freedom and justice. While the Romanovs' collapse in 1917 was triggered by the colossal pressures of World War I, it had been prepared by centuries of accumulated grievances and the monarchy's repeated failures to address them meaningfully.

As this book concludes, we are left with a complex tapestry of sorrow, resilience, and unfulfilled hopes. Russia's historical reliance on fear-based rule reveals how authoritarian methods can stifle progress and provoke violent backlash. Yet this same history offers glimpses of alternative paths—moments of reform, communal innovation, and cultural flourishing. Whether under the aegis of a tsar, or in any other form of governance, the persistent question remains: Can a nation so large and diverse find a way to unify without oppression? The Romanov era's tragic ending stands as a cautionary tale of what happens when a ruling class believes fear alone can guarantee order, and of how swiftly such an order can crumble when faith in authority disappears.

Help Us Share Your Thoughts!

Dear reader,

Thank you for spending your time with this book. We hope it brought you enjoyment and a few new ideas to think about. If there was anything that didn't work for you, or if you have suggestions on how we can improve, please let us know at **kontakt@skriuwer.com**. Your feedback means a lot to us and helps us make our books even better.

If you enjoyed this book, we would be very grateful if you left a review on the site where you purchased it. Your review not only helps other readers find our books, but also encourages us to keep creating more stories and materials that you'll love.

By choosing Skriuwer, you're also supporting **Frisian**—a minority language mainly spoken in the northern Netherlands. Although **Frisian** has a rich history, the number of speakers is shrinking, and it's at risk of dying out. Your purchase helps fund resources to preserve and promote this language, such as educational programs and learning tools. If you'd like to learn more about Frisian or even start learning it yourself, please visit **www.learnfrisian.com**.

Thank you for being part of our community. We look forward to sharing more books with you in the future.

Warm regards,
The Skriuwer Team

Printed in Great Britain
by Amazon